# SHE WHO PAYS

# SHE WHO PAYS

by

## MRS ROBERT HENREY

For Colby Womens College
Library
New Hampshire
from
Madeleine Henrey

Feb. 1975

LONDON
J. M. DENT & SONS LTD

Made in Great Britain
at the
Aldine Press · Letchworth · Herts
for
J. M. DENT & SONS LTD
Aldine House · Bedford Street · London
First published 1969

SBN: 460 03894 x

He that pryeth into every cloud may be
stricken with a thunderbolt.

*English proverb.*

# CONTENTS

# THE THUNDERBOLT

# I

ACHANCE remark did it, a minimum of words whispered in my ear by a man who had no reason, and probably no intention, to hurt me. In the time that it takes to glance at a map, something which I had until then believed to be a positive insurance against adversity, a thing of unlimited duration was seemingly to be arbitrarily taken away from me. As my entire future could not help but be grievously affected, and not only my future but that of others, my peace of mind was absurdly, unbelievably shattered.

Saturday morning of Easter week! The air was crisp, the sun had come out after breakfast and I was probably feeling too sure of myself. One waits the whole winter through for spring; and when it comes, when the hedgerows are full of primroses, the orchards of cowslips, the garden of daffodils, tulips and narcissi, one has a right to feel a childish elation. I had driven down from the farm with some violets (the hedges were full of them, but these were dark and strongly scented from the garden) for friends who had just opened their villa by the sea for the Easter holidays.

I left my car for a moment in front of one of the fish stalls in the market. I was just edging my way into the newspaper shop, always crowded at this hour, where the girls put aside for me every morning my mail and the newspapers, when a neighbouring landowner, after the usual politenesses, said to me in rather an urgent voice: 'Have you seen the blueprint of the new fast motorway planned eventually to by-pass the village? It cuts right through your land. Ask somebody at the town hall to show it you. I'll try to arrange for one of the town councillors to produce it for you on Monday if you like.'

Right through my land, I thought, glancing at the headlines on the front page of the Paris edition of the *New York Herald Tribune*. That might mean almost anywhere. A road, as long as it went through distant orchards, seemed a fairly nebulous threat. As my neighbour's tall figure cast a shadow behind me I turned in annoyance from the newspaper which, in spite of the coming and going in the tiny shop, I was trying to read, and said to the bearer of bad news: 'Thanks for telling me, but don't bother. I'll go over myself some time.'

I needed to talk this over—but not with a stranger, not with somebody who might notice how secretly perturbed I was. I saw my husband coming back from the baker with two long French loaves, and we went straight to the town hall which was exactly opposite the paper shop. The local schoolmaster came thoughtfully down the stairs. One of us said to him: 'Is it true there's a map or a blueprint of the new motorway?'

We were pretty certain that M. Salesse would know because he was a town councillor. There was another reason, a personal one, why he would know about the road.

One winter afternoon, when a bitter north wind was sweeping across a grey, sullen beach, we found M. Salesse on the front staring in the direction of England. We stopped the car to inquire after his health and to ask him what he was thinking about. Some years earlier he had built himself a small house on what we called the road to St Vaast, though it was less a road than a country lane. Indeed by some miracle the lane had remained much as it was when I had first known it some thirty years earlier: a sweetly unexpected winding, up-hill-down-dale, lonely road whose hedges, heavy with the scent of violets and cowslips, bushy with hazel, were ennobled at intervals by the tall majesty of elm and oak. This lane swept like a protecting arm round the eastern confines of three agricultural estates: that of Andrée Pradeau, whose father, Dr Salmont, owned 'Bois Lurette', a Russian *dacha*-type house immortalized by the Impressionist painters at the end of the last century; a very fine farm leased by our immediate neighbours, the Levanniers, from the widow of a notary, Maître Bompain; and so on until it embraced a long stretch of my own land, a piece that we called the Picane, and which was the most distant from our house.

To return to M. Salesse. His little house was on the opposite side of the lane from that which bordered the main bodies of the estates I have just mentioned. It stood back from the lane, almost hidden by trees, and its garden communicated with that of an

extremely pretty old-world cottage that had originally belonged
to his parents and which was now the home of his mother-in-law,
Mme Javot, a busy, obliging, energetic little woman with whom
my mother during her last years had been very friendly. Mme
Javot used to collect my mother's new-laid eggs every morning
and sell them for her at market.

M. Salesse thought of his new house as a place in which he
would retire. Just now he was lodged in the village school where
he was head of the boys' side and his wife head of the girls' side,
and his daughter, married to an assistant master, head of the
infants' school. Soon they would all be grouped on either side
of the road to St Vaast, the schoolmaster having recently purchased
from Maître Bompain's widow a piece of land on which he was
building a house for his daughter and son-in-law.

I had watched the progress of his daughter's house that winter
when digging the rude earth or tending the hedge in my kitchen
garden. The hedge from which all the fine trees had been cut
divided my kitchen garden from M. Levannier's very large home
orchard, a piece of land which extended all the way from Cathedral
Lane to the road to St Vaast. M. Levannier's large brick house,
his many barns, cider press and stables were grouped at one end,
all the rest being cider apple trees and grazing land. It was this
latter part that my kitchen garden overlooked, a beautiful
undulating view with distant glimpses of Mount Canisy.

The Levanniers who had replaced Ernest and Yvonne Poulin
on this neighbouring farm were young, modern and purposeful.
They had two small children, a boy and a girl, dressed whenever
we saw them that winter in bright red, who trotted after their
parents like woodland pixies. The Levanniers were here to
wring everything they could out of the rich soil and to put
enough money aside to buy land of their own, possibly in the
Eure where their parents had a farm. We liked their directness
and frank, open faces. They were something entirely new, leaving
us with only a dimming memory of the Norman peasants we
had known thirty years earlier who, with their cunning and
deviousness, their sorcery and scheming and double talk, their
partiality for cider and apple-jack which caused so many tragic
hangings in cider presses, made them characters out of Maupas-
sant, earthy, greedy and picturesque. I doubt if the Levanniers
often drank anything much stronger than water, and they were

the sort of people who thought nothing of locking up their house after the cows had been milked in the morning and going off for the day, perhaps to see their parents, only returning at seven o'clock in time for the evening milking.

The Levanniers, however, were the first to shock us quite unintentionally with their methods.

The hedges between orchards, hedges once so shady and luxurious, when dividing one person's land from another's, belong erratically to one or the other according to tradition which may be several centuries old. Though nearly all my land, through patience and good fortune, is contiguous, it so happens that my home orchard (the one on which my house is situated) has orchards belonging to Mme Bompain along two sides of it. When first I bought the farm, Ernest Poulin, who was incredibly well versed in local usage and old Norman law, had revealed to me, by the aid of half-hidden stone boundary marks, what lengths of these hedges were mine and what others were his. A hedge, for instance, after meandering half way between two orchards can suddenly cease to be yours and belong to your neighbour, and then, beyond a wild cherry tree or an elm, suddenly change ownership a second time. Ernest Poulin used to say that when a hedge was yours it carried with it one and a half metres of land on the other side. These rights and privileges were jealously guarded all the way down the ages from the time of William the Conqueror.

Well, it was Mr Levannier's theory that bushy hedges, in which here and there tall trees grow, rob an orchard of some valuable inches of pasture land. Nobody believed any longer, of course, that any farmer would consider it a paying proposition to limit his livestock, as his forefathers had done, to one cow for every two acres of land. The idea was to pack as many animals as possible on to every available inch of grass, and if bushy hedges with trees in them threw shade and damp on grass verges, off with the heads of the hedges!

Concurrently with these ideas that had already destroyed so many hedgerows in England, Norman farmers no longer attached an almost religious importance to their cider apple trees.

Were we not taught at school that the Druids worshipped mistletoe? When I first came here Norman peasants had that sort of feeling for everything appertaining to the cider apple—and even for the little hard pears that dropped like gold from those tall aged trees and which, when distilled, made potent and much appreciated pear-jack.

When I bought the farm the long thatched cider presses, most of them centuries old, were still places of hushed speech and strange rites—a sort of private Stonehenge on every farm, a place of midnight invoking, scheming, plotting, hanging, sometimes even murder. The immense vats in the cool semi-darkness of those high raftered rooms were tended and felt and tapped, and the nectar was tasted from an unhygienic tumbler a hundred times a day. My farmer Goguet used so often to walk from his house to the cider press down by the river that his steps each season wore down the grass.

It might be an exaggeration to say that nobody in these parts drank cider any more, but it had become so little a part of their lives that M. Levannier was cutting down his cider trees by the hundred, and even being paid by the government for doing so. Young farmers of his generation who did not drink cider themselves, or only very occasionally, wanted the grass of which each apple tree in a thickly planted orchard robbed them. In its efforts to combat alcoholism the government allowed owners the equivalent of about a pound for every cider apple tree cut down, the money being made available in the form of a grant against the putting up of new farm buildings. Thus, as I dug up my potatoes in the kitchen garden, I had the previous winter watched the massacre of long lines of cider apple trees in M. Levannier's orchard, trees that Ernest Poulin had so lovingly planted thirty years earlier.

I had grown to dislike the sound of the electric saw. Its long, shrill whine had a devastating effect on my nerves. To hear a young tree crashing down gave me also the same feeling of impotent revolt as to see one of our cats bringing a baby rabbit into the garden. I longed to rescue it and give it life again.

Our house is in the centre of a six-acre rectangular orchard which descends gently from the white gate at the top to one of those meandering, crystal-clear streams that in this part of the country have their source one never quite knows where, and disappear a mile or so farther along just as mysteriously. The lane at the top of my home orchard starts in front of M. Levannier's red brick house and circumscribes an oasis of my own land, very small, about five acres, tongue-shaped and elevated. At the far end of it is 'Berlequet', the house I lease to my tenant farmer Jacques Déliquaire, with its stables, cowsheds, garden and cider press. We call this oasis the Pointe because of its elongated shape. Part of its northern end rises almost clifflike and is then surmounted by a plateau of beautiful rich grass from which one has a sweeping view of the country all around, from the sea facing the English coast to a fine French château to the south.

Few people use this lane except ourselves, our farmers and the Levanniers who, as I have already said, have an orchard on either side of the one in which we have our house. But tradition has it that the hedge nearest my white entrance gate is theirs and not mine, and to my horror one winter's day a very pleasant man called M. Paris, who occasionally did odd jobs for the Levanniers, arrived at their request to cut down the hedge along the two hundred-odd yards over which Mme Bompain had jurisdiction.

I hoped, of course, that it would merely be trimmed, as hedges must be every seven years, but this one emerged from the operation like a man who had walked into a barber's shop and had his head shaved as bald as an egg. After everything had been cut and shaved and felled M. Levannier arrived, gay, debonair and charming, to run up barbed wire between stakes. I felt terrible, but after all it was none of my business. He said gaily: 'These darned hedges, stealing the grass from my cattle. As soon as I have time I'll cut down every single one of them over which tradition gives me a right.'

He was far too nice a man to quarrel with, and I loved to see the Levanniers milking their cows of an evening with the two little red pixies chasing each other over the grass. But perhaps I sensed that this was the beginning of the end, though neither my husband nor I could have guessed that these were indeed trifling vexations compared with the magnitude of what would soon engulf us—and not only us, but the Levanniers and the Déliquaires and everybody else in this earthly paradise.

The young farmers themselves in pursuing their objectives could not reasonably be blamed. Nor were they aware of the other more sinister forces rumbling all about them. The fact is that everything, everywhere, was on the move.

But of course I didn't see it at the time. One never does. I, like so many other allegedly well-informed people, kept tilting at windmills.

My own farmer's seven-year lease was due for renewal. Generally speaking, this was a mere formality, an exchange of signatures before a notary, such documents being very one-sided affairs. No landowner these days can get rid of a tenant farmer against his will, even at the end of a lease—not that I had any desire to see Jacques Déliquaire go. His father had been my tenant and I had known him since as a little boy he trotted across the orchards with my son. Besides, I always looked forward to a good gossip with his wife Georgette, who brought me the milk every other day. I had never regretted giving them the farm.

The hedge that M. Levannier had massacred beside my white entrance gate tormented me so much that I asked permission to insert a clause in my own farmer's new lease to the effect that hedges must not be trimmed beyond the old-fashioned custom of the country. I meant by this that trees, of course, must not be cut down and that pollards and hazels should not be trimmed below the height of a man. Jacques Déliquaire made no objection to the insertion of this clause, pointing out that this was merely what he always did.

My attempt to save our hedges, a matter of great concern to me, was probably futile. In the damp lanes between orchards there were places where cowslips, violets and wood strawberries abounded, where in autumn one picked blackberries and hazel-nuts, but these had become rare. The white campion, shepherd's purse, sandwort, wild mignonette, field pansy and ragged robin were still reasonably common. The real trouble was that over the last twenty years trees in hedges that died were never replaced, hazel was cut too low and never grew up again, holly and wild rose almost completely disappeared, and all the beautiful, sweet-smelling miracles of nature were replaced by barbed wire and stinging-nettles. This, of course, gave a farmer an excuse for spraying the nettles with poison and leaving nothing but the barbed wire and a few tufts of green.

The hedge between my kitchen garden and the pasture land of M. Levannier's home field belonged to him. No trees were left in it but tall, tough elders and an undergrowth of nettles in which lay hidden old pots and broken bottles dating from Ernest Poulin's time, and even earlier for all I know, when the hedge had been used by both houses for what could neither be fed to chickens nor destroyed by fire. With Levannier's approbation we trimmed the overhanging branches of elder and removed from the hedge soil the deep yellow roots of the stinging nettles and everything that had been thrown into it. To what extent did country folk centuries back plan the hedgerows that we are so busy destroying today? Did they plant the elm and the wild cherry? Did they or nature add the wild violet and the primrose, the cowslip, the wood strawberry and the hazel? Our particular area, though rich in cowslips and violets, had few primroses. Our nearness to the sea could not have been the reason, because they grew abundantly in hedges much nearer the sands than ours only two or three miles farther along the coast. But they thrived best and in such quantities as I had never seen them before near a small village called Beaumont-en-Auge, where certain lanes were riotous with primroses and periwinkles from February onwards so that the air was heavy with their scent.

With the approval of farmers who were on the point of cutting down their hedges, we decided to dig up some of the primroses while they were in early flower and bring them back in the car. Could we transform our arid hedge into something as infinitely beautiful as it had undoubtedly been a century ago? Each plant was dug up with about two pounds of its own soil and dropped into our own hedge within half an hour of its removal. The first year we planted two hundred and all of them flourished, so that we kept on adding year by year, until we had about four hundred in all, not to speak of violets, celandine, cowslips and wood strawberries.

But nobody was any longer in the business to improve the looks of the countryside. All winter M. Levannier kept heifers and young bulls on this part of his home orchard. They roamed its vastness between the stumps of the cider apple trees felled the previous autumn. The grass had long ago been churned by the animals' hooves into slime. One could hardly believe that grass would ever grow there again. It would, of course, and be more beautiful than ever. Just now the animals were hungry and high spirited. I am not quite sure why, but it was at 4 p.m. every day that the herd arrived opposite our kitchen garden. Three things brought them there: our presence in the garden, for animals love the company of human beings; the bark of the elder trees; and, most important of all, the lush grass and tender wild flowers on our side of the hedge.

These beautiful young animals, with large loving eyes and more appealing lashes than any girl can buy at a ten-cent store and stick over her own, would dare one another to clamber and slither up their muddy side of the hedge and peek through the barbed wire at all the goodies to eat on our side. It took less than a second for a pink tongue to flick over a tender primrose plant. Young, agile and full of energy, they stood on top of the hedge bank and in impossibly precarious positions chewed off the bark of the elder trees and thrust their heads through the taut barbed wire in the hope of breaking it. Soon the elder trees looked as if they had been blasted by gunfire. Not a scrap of bark remained. A piece of barbed wire snapped and I looked up from my spade to see a young heifer trotting across the strawberry beds. The damage that cattle can do in a kitchen garden is considerable. And how do you propose to get them out?

M. Levannier was delightfully apologetic. Would you like to claim from my insurance? Can I bring you some feed for your hens? I'll put up another strand of barbed wire. We talked amicably across the fence. The cutting down of his apple trees gave us a distant view of the sea and some low violet hills, Mount Canisy half way to Deauville. The house M. Salesse was building for his daughter and son-in-law shone in the afternoon light. The roof would soon be on.

This lower part of Levannier's home field was both large and fertile. To the south it stretched away to a beautiful narrow lane which separated it from Andrée Pradeau's magnificent property, 'Bois Lurette', while to the east it was bordered by the road to St Vaast. It was at the junction of the Pradeaus' park and the road to St Vaast that the house was going up, and I allowed myself to ask a question that had intrigued me.

'How was Mme Bompain able to dispose of that corner of your home orchard? Didn't it form part of your leased acreage?'

'Why yes,' said M. Levannier reasonably, 'but I had no cause to prevent her from selling it if that was her desire. We get along very well together, and, when I've wanted something, she has invariably met me more than half way.'

This in itself was one of the nicer facets of relations between landowners and young farmers, but I said with a touch of malice:

'When you wanted to cut down all those cider apple trees, for instance?'

A tenant farmer cannot cut down a tree without the owner's permission.

M. Levannier was not a bit annoyed by my question. His face, on the contrary, took a joyous expression and he said:

'Oh, but I was right. As soon as I can find the time I'll bring along the tractor and pull all the roots up. Then in summer you'll see what a fine meadow it will make.' He smiled indulgently and added: 'I'm not such a vandal as you think. I've left hundreds of trees at the bottom of the orchard. But this meadow will give me grass for my small animals. See how I've trimmed the southern hedge, the one over against the Pradeaus' place. I swear it will give me an extra three yards of grass all the way along. One can't afford to waste pasture or farm haphazardly any longer. Profit margins are too small.'

'I know,' I answered. 'Nobody can criticize you. Nobody would dare to. You represent the new ideas. Will you try one day to buy this land from Mme Bompain? Isn't there a law that prevents a landowner from selling a piece of agricultural land without first offering it to his tenant farmer?'

'I would not buy it,' said M. Levannier.

'Why not?' I asked. 'You're not the sort of people to remain tenants all your lives. You're too ambitious, too energetic, too modern.'

'Of course we aim to have a farm of our own,' said M. Levannier. 'Perhaps in nine or ten years. When we have had time to put some money aside. But not here. The price of land here is uneconomic and, as the price that a farmer is paid for his livestock is controlled, I would be a fool not to go where land is cheaper. It's entirely unrealistic to value land, as it's valued here, at a fancy price just because we are near Deauville.'

'We are in the famous Pays d'Auge,' I said.

M. Levannier shrugged his shoulders. 'That was fine in the old days,' he said. 'It doesn't count any longer now. Even farm rents here are uneconomic. My wife and I do all the work. We even milk the cows ourselves. It's rare that I employ a man even to help me cut a hedge. You would be surprised at the end of the year how little we can put aside.'

In saying that he was perhaps exaggerating, but he was right about the price of the land. His land and mine and that of the Pradeaus, and in fact all the land hereabouts, was supposed to be worth for agricultural purposes between £750 and £850 an acre, though it never came up for sale. Yes, M. Levannier was right. He would have been stupid to pay that sort of price. And it was a myth anyway, I reflected. What would happen if one of us tried to sell?

It was not long after this that we had stopped the car on that bitter afternoon to talk to M. Salesse, who was on the front staring out across a sullen sea in the direction of England.

The main road from Deauville to Caen follows the sea coast until it reaches the bottom of our village. Here it suddenly describes an acute left-hand turn to proceed in a straight line up a steep hill on its way to Houlgate, Dives and Cabourg.

Now for almost as long as I can remember there had been vague talk about by-passing our village. Fast new motorways were being built all over France. The country was being sliced up to give added impetus to the nationalized car industry.

From time to time, mostly out of politeness, I would ask the notables of the village—the notary, the mayor, the councillors—if there was any news about the proposed road. On one occasion rumour had it that the plan was merely to cut off the abrupt left-hand turn by a short by-pass that would branch off the present road some two miles in front of our village and rejoin it some two miles beyond it. The Pradeaus had been told that it might traverse the roundabout in front of the big white gates leading to their estate. So many other roads were being built that nobody worried. A new express motorway between Paris and Deauville would not be finished for another eighteen months at least. A new fast road starting from Tancarville, the great bridge across the mouth of the Seine, had already sliced away the extreme top of the road to St Vaast, and the traffic along it was so sparse that one wondered why it had been necessary to build a road at all, especially at the cost of such unusually valuable farmland. Was not France essentially an agricultural country? Would future generations not regret, perhaps, the spoliation of the Pays d'Auge, richest dairy land in Europe, comparable with the best in New Zealand?

On that cold winter afternoon, I said to M. Salesse:

'Have you any news about the road, M. Salesse?'

He looked up, considered my question a moment and it struck me that he was preoccupied. 'I'm hoping to retire in a few years,' he said. 'I sincerely hope that it won't pass too near my house. It would spoil the peace of our beautiful valley. And just think of the noise!'

What he said about the road passing near his house puzzled me. The noise of a great arterial road can carry quite a distance—a quarter of a mile perhaps. But an uneasy suspicion was rising in my mind.

'Would it affect you as badly as that', I asked, 'if the road were to pass, as rumour has it, in front of the white gates of the Pradeau estate? After all, there's an avenue of trees nearly four hundred yards in length before one even reaches their house. And that's a quarter of a mile from you.'

'You refer to the original blueprint,' said M. Salesse. 'There's a more recent one. The road would pass above the Pradeau estate, not below it.'

'You mean——?'

'Yes, exactly. I'm very much in the danger area, I fear. Very near indeed.'

'It might then pass quite close to your house and to your mother-in-law's cottage and to the house you are building for your daughter and son-in-law?'

'Quite close. Much too close, though it would actually cross the present road to St Vaast a little farther along. Near the transformer, I think.'

'Then in order to link up with the road to Caen it would need to pass over part of my land?'

M. Salesse raised his arms in a gesture full of significance.

'Oh well,' I said, 'if it eventually takes place I shall doubtless lose a piece of my Picane. There's nothing I can do about it. When are they supposed to start work?'

'Not this year or next year,' said M. Salesse. 'They've got to find the money first.'

We talked about other things. There really didn't seem much
to worry about.

De Gaulle's France, judging by our village, seemed immensely
prosperous. The salaries of the 'cadres', or business executives,
and the vertiginous rise in the purchase value of Paris apartments,
that brought immense fortunes to speculators, no longer even
surprised us. Several pages of the *Figaro* were every day devoted
to the details of new skyscraper apartment houses that were
christened by such names as Marie Antoinette Domain. People
in conversation bandied millions about, millions of old francs,
each million being roughly worth the equivalent of one thousand
pounds. 'My apartment will cost me nearly fifty thousand pounds!'
Our coastline was suffering a change, but in a different way.
A great wave of snobbery had hit the nation. Up till now we
had enjoyed every summer the gaudy picturesqueness and the
appalling litter of the caravan site. The town councils of the
poorer Paris suburbs took over erstwhile private châteaux and
estates for summer holiday camps. The seaside hotel, which no
longer seemed to have a place in modern French society,
gave up, and became a holiday house for the state electricity
concern, a motor works or a chemical factory. Some were used
for retired workers and their families; others for the workers
themselves. Children, led by paid students on semi-vacation,
marched in long crocodiles through the lanes and down to the
beach singing the 'Internationale' and occasionally, as during
Léon Blum's Popular Front in 1938, waving the Red Flag.
But now, in this land of constant contradiction, the snob
thing for those who lived in town was to have what became known
as a 'secondary residence'. Two cars for a family, three if there
was a son at college, whisky for anybody who looked in, and a
secondary residence, were modern necessities.
The secondary residence was another little gold-mine to be
exploited by speculators. To us, who had so far escaped it, the
fever to build was fanned by the whispered assurance that as
soon as the new Paris–Deauville motorway was completed, the
126 miles that separated the two cities could be covered by a
modern fast car in an hour and a half. Already two or three
sections alone remained unfinished.
All this agitation was not immediately discernible to those who,

like myself, were primarily concerned with feminine duties such as washing and ironing, dusting and cleaning, tending the rose trees and digging the kitchen garden, making jam and apple jelly, all without the help of a maid or even a daily. But apart from my frequent trips to the village I was kept adequately informed of what was going on by Georgette, our farmer's young wife, whose little girl Brigitte now went to college at Deauville. With her also I was able to smooth over recurring problems that occasionally bedevil an estate.

It was natural that our village should be growing.

For quite a time the low ground down by the sea, like the outskirts of any English seaside town, had been sprouting new bungalows. In this area were the gasworks, the tennis courts, a few market gardens and one or two shops at the corners of streets that were not yet finished. Bordering the sandgrit highway overlooking the Channel was a great marshy field which in summer, when the ground became dry, was magically turned into one of the largest caravan sites along the coast.

Farther back on higher ground stood the brightly painted, toylike railway station, the hillside cemetery and an avenue of plane trees leading back to the village. Along this avenue, at the corner of a housing estate, the police station was to be transferred from its present position in the village centre behind the town hall and the market-place.

We had always taken it for granted that this was the direction in which our village would expand. Presumably it would one day join up with Deauville, just as, on the opposite side of the Channel, Rottingdean had long ago joined up with Brighton. The people who bought houses on the low ground were mostly of modest means, foremen in the building trade, electricians, house painters and retired couples.

Wealthier families lived on the cliffs on the other side of the village or had fine houses, some dating from the gay nineties, with musical comedy towers and turrets. Some were new and reputedly worth not less than thirty thousand pounds, solidly built with English-type lawns and rockeries. These were on the steeply rising road that led up from the post office and the notary's house to the white gates of the Pradeau estate. That was where the new road was originally to have cut across.

From here along Cathedral Lane were what had once been impressive country seats, each with a large house, a finely wooded park, a private farm and sufficient acres of pasture land to graze a small herd. These were the homes of the famous and the rich. Only two were now in private hands—the Pradeau estate and one which belonged to a member of the Michelin family. The others were in the process of suffering a mighty change.

Beyond this area on the plateau was the real, productive farmland on which farmers like the Levanniers and the Déliquaires toiled youthfully and happily for a living. Here, one might almost say, was the backbone of the province known the world over for its butter and its cheese.

The Pradeau park, its sheep pens and private farm ran along the whole of one side of Cathedral Lane as far as Levanniers' solid brick farmhouse. Yes, indeed, the Pradeau estate was a joy, and Andrée Pradeau the most delightful and gifted young *châtelaine*.

On the other side of the lane was the 'Pelouses', an estate which in the old days must have been quite as beautiful. The house of noble proportions overlooked a vast, sweeping meadow where the Victorian owners must have sauntered in summer with their guests. When the glory of the 'Pelouses' departed the farm which had formed part of the estate passed into the hands of the Bellays, whose widow now farmed its small acreage on her own. The farmhouse was half-timbered, slated and several hundred years old—probably sixteenth century. So were the cider press and outhouses. The orchard in which they stood had one gate opening on Cathedral Lane and another on the present Deauville–Caen highway. At some point along this highway, people said, the new by-pass would eventually link up.

The 'Pelouses' itself had even before my time suffered the fate of Victorian houses which eventually proved too large for the families occupying them. The Socialist town council of a Paris suburb bought it as a summer holiday home for workers' children. They looked healthy and moderately content to find themselves in such quiet surroundings. Then one summer they didn't come. More suitable premises were found elsewhere—in Brittany, I think. The 'Pelouses' was advertised for sale in the *Figaro* newspaper and we were not a little astonished to read that the asking price was in the neighbourhood of seventy-five thousand pounds!

For what reason would a purchaser be willing to pay such a fabulous figure?

People began to suspect that the reason might lie in what was just then happening to yet another of these formerly proud estates. The Château de San Carlo, originally owned by the Countess of Béarn, practically adjoined the 'Pelouses' and also had an entrance gate on the Caen highway. A quiet road, bordered by magnificent chestnut trees, ran alongside the grounds and led from the highway (at the corner of which stood the lodge) to the roundabout opposite the leafy semi-obscurity of Cathedral Lane. In the countess's day her road was closed at both ends at night to any but her own carriages to ensure peace and quiet.

'Château' was a high sounding appellation for this ornate, high-ceilinged French country house with its stone terrace and steps leading down to the lawn, its faint air of romanticism, evoking tea parties, young girls in white blouses and ankle-length skirts, games of tennis, bicycling and horse-riding, and shrimping down by the black cliffs. The house suffered the inevitable metamorphosis into apartments for sale. Who would not have a 'château' for an address?

The park was cut up into lots upon which purchasers were invited to have built to their design a pseudo-Norman, reed-thatched, half-timbered *chaumière* (the word was madly in the wind) like various exhibition ones that seemed to vary in price between £9,500 and £13,000, which included the small plots of ground on which they were built. How many such dolls' houses standing in their little handkerchiefs of land could be squeezed into this area? Every third or fourth chestnut tree along the road bore a nailed notice defacing its trunk: 'Lot No. –'. For one more year perhaps these noble trees would be allowed to burst into leaf and light up the countryside with their rosy chandeliers, the finest spectacle of May. However, as each lot was sold along came the electric saw. 'Lot No. 23' . . . 'Lot No. 24' . . . 'Lot No. 25' . . . Down they would crash like traitors executed by a firing squad.

The 'Pelouses', in spite of the advertisement in the paper, was not immediately sold. The asking price may have been a little high, though who could tell these days when millions slipped so easily off the tongue? People assumed, however, that its fate would be similar to that of San Carlo. Meanwhile cows were turned out to graze on its sloping meadow, and when spring arrived periwinkles peeped out from the tufted bank under the tall trees of Cathedral Lane. M. Paris, the steward, a very good-looking man (the girls of his family were famous for their beauty), wondered vaguely what would happen to him when the place was sold. Meanwhile he continued to cut hedges for neighbouring farmers and in autumn to help them gather in the cider apples. He worked with the ease and precision of former generations. He offered us several cords of elm, ash and cherry in four-foot lengths and stacked them beautifully in rows at the back of the stables. Men of his calibre had become rare.

Suddenly an even more exciting piece of news reached us. The widow Bellay, at the request of her children, was selling her farm. So it looked as if that might go before the big house to which it had once been attached.

Mme Bellay was a friendly, vivacious little woman who had known our house long before we bought it. Since the death of her husband she had managed the fourteen-odd acres of orchard and meadow alone. Every time I drove along Cathedral Lane I peeped at her beautiful, half-timbered house, the washing on the line and her few cows and chickens.

For her farmhouse, her cider press, her stables, outhouses and well-planted orchards she was asking what seemed a lot of money. But nobody in the village seemed to think so. The fact was that it was a farm and it wasn't. As a farm the acreage was too small to make it economic. As a house, as pretty as a picture, renovated and modernized, the possibilities so near the village and the sea were, to say the least, intriguing, but who would have the imagination and ready cash to buy it?

People still appeared boisterously prosperous, proud to be told on television that France, under General de Gaulle, was setting such a shining example to other nations, especially America and Britain. France balanced her budget, kept income tax relatively low, filled the coffers of the Bank of France with gold brought triumphantly from the United States—a nation gravely menaced by political assassinations, colour problems and a war in Vietnam. Britain also should learn to put its house in order, prevent the pound from being further devalued, and make itself worthy of joining the Common Market. France was strong,

peace-loving and the ideal arbiter in a troubled world. Who
else but the General could go to Moscow and be so enthusiastic-
ally acclaimed? What other great nation was financially so strong
that it could allow its citizens freely to buy gold bars and coins?

Our friends, the Laurents, found their house in the village
noisy.

They had therefore bought a very pretty house at Vauville, a
tiny village some eight or nine miles inland. The house had a
dreamy, fairy-like quality that might have made it the setting of a
nineteenth-century novel. A romantic stone archway led from
the road into a courtyard on either side of which were half-
timbered granges of exceptional beauty. There was a kitchen
garden bordered by a cool stream. Annette Laurent was delighted,
even though the property would cost nearly as much to modernize
as to purchase. But it would prove an absolute jewel, and a
policeman and his wife would inhabit an entirely delightful lodge.
Workmen and stonemasons would be moving in immediately,
and she hoped to have the place ready for a house-warming by
Christmas. She would try to drive down from her Paris apartment
most week-ends to supervise the work.

Would they come as often to the sands when they lived eight
miles inland? Would we have fewer friends in summer on the
beach? Meanwhile who would buy the Bellay farm that in its
different way was nearly as romantic as the house at Vauville?

With all this money floating round, how desperately poor I
suddenly felt!

Until this year we had never quite got round to making the
best out of spring. The metamorphosis of the hedge that separated
our kitchen garden from the lower part of M. Levannier's home
orchard was only part of our determination to see our house
surrounded by spring flowers. With the exception of a few clumps
of wild daffodils that grew by some extraordinary mistake in one
of our more distant orchards, the Cour du Cerf, we would
normally see fewer daffodils, narcissi and tulips in and around our
village than I saw every spring on costers' barrows in London.
Perhaps one gets sentimental from seeing them in Chelsea
window-boxes, in carefully prepared beds in Hyde Park or round
the older houses in Shepherd Market—or again it may come from
reading too much Victorian literature.

Our farmers were not really flower-minded at all. Their wives may have been in a sporadic unactive way, but the men were certainly not. They were too busy on their tractors, and it no longer even amused them to keep up those small kitchen gardens that were a feature of every farmhouse when we first bought our own. Ernest Poulin had a lovely one, for instance, with peach trees and espalier pears but his successor, M. Levannier, had allowed it to become a wilderness. He said, 'I simply haven't the time', as if farmers in the old days worked less hard, which is not what everybody would have us believe. Jacques Déliquaire, our own tenant farmer, had not thought it worth while to go on with the one that his predecessor, M. Groscol, so lovingly tended. Jacques grew a few potatoes and lettuces in front of his house, but often Georgette found it easier to open a tin of peas from the supermarket.

The previous autumn I had written to the various Dutch producers to send me, through their French agents, numerous bulbs of different kinds. We planted them wherever we thought the cows would not chew them up (as they invariably did the wild daffodils in the Cour du Cerf), but chiefly in front of the house and in wide beds in the kitchen garden. Rather to our surprise, they all flourished in successive waves of beauty and colour—the snowdrops, the daffodils, the narcissi, single and double, and every sort of tulip from fat scarlet ones that came out early to those with delicate heads on long, elegant stems.

I was only now beginning to realize the difference that the superfluous makes. My beautiful Christmas trees, for instance, were quite useless from a farming viewpoint, but were heavenly at this time of year with their tender green sprouts and the half-light between their tall, straight trunks, their carpet of needles through which grew lilies-of-the-valley and wood strawberries, and now patches of primroses! The peasants, and I use the word advisedly, cunning, picturesque and lovable, whom we had had the good fortune to know, though only on the verge of their disappearance, had, of course, been much more at one with the land. They had practically formed a part of it. While a man was making faggots down by the stream he would pause to meditate on the sky, the birds or the little wild flowers that grew along the mossy bank. They knew every tree by name, the cries of the different owls, even where they lived. They knew where to find the best nuts, the juiciest blackberries. Times were hard, and each thing that nature gave them was of value.

The previous autumn, when one bright cold morning I went out with a basket to gather blackberries for jam making, I found that my tenant farmer had sprayed all the loveliest autumnal hedges with chemicals—to kill the blackberry bushes, the wild rose and the hips and haws.

'Oh,' I cried, 'couldn't you at least have thought of my jam! We live on it all the winter.'

In one of his rare moments of anger he answered: 'Do you suppose I have the time to cut the hedges by hand? This is the modern way. In a month all the brambles will wither and die!'

How can one get into a state of not caring about the heritage that after all does not belong to any one person? While the Levanniers were cutting down apple trees I planted walnut trees to give shade to the cows where the hedges were thin. At other places I planted edible chestnut trees so that when the cold weather came we could roast them or make *marrons glacés*. Every January till recently we replaced the cider apple trees that were dead from old age or had fallen during the gales with different varieties of eating-apple trees. One had to think of this in terms of the next generation, of trying to hand on in excellent state what during a lifetime one had learned to love and appreciate. The planting of fruit trees is expensive. The government didn't pay one for planting them, only for cutting them down. Also there was always a certain heartache when the cows came, because, in spite of the steel corsets with which one protected the young trunks, milk cows are so tall, and occasionally so vicious, not against people but against foliage, that they will resort to acrobatics to tear the young grafted shoots off newly planted fruit trees, so that the work of several years may be ruined in a moment. One learns to hide one's resentment—but resentment against whom, against what? The cows? They were like children. I loved them. So one planted new trees.

'At least my son may benefit,' I thought whenever the question came up.


On Saturday mornings we took to going to market at Dives, which was only twenty minutes' drive by car. The Saturday morning market there is one of the loveliest and most picturesque in this part of the world.

It is from Dives that William the Conqueror in 1066 is supposed to have set out with fifty thousand men-at-arms and two hundred thousand other ranks on his conquest of England. Over the entrance of the fourteenth-century church is a list of the principal soldiers in the Conqueror's expeditionary force.

The church and fifteenth-century wooden market hall are fortunately by-passed by the main road to Caen, so that one needs to be aware of their existence, and the narrow, colourful street that connects them is closed to traffic on market day so that one can saunter peacefully past the shops and stalls, sniffing the freshly baked bread, the *croissants* and buttery, golden *brioches*. Periodically we bought young laying hens from one or other of the peasant women who still brought butter, eggs, vegetables and fowls from their own farms, but on the whole the once familiar sight of the farmers' wives seated on camp-stools beside their produce is disappearing. The co-operatives tend nowadays to collect the produce of each farm morning and evening, and in these circumstances most farmers sell their milk in bulk without even bothering to make butter or cream for themselves.

In the open market square the ruins of the abbey of Ste Marie du Hibou overlook the stalls of the cheese vendors and the plants and shrubs set out by the nurserymen. I found it pleasant in this medieval setting to re-create with story-book simplicity days gone by—the Conqueror's seaport with the loading and unloading of vessels, the hammer blows of shipwrights and so on, until in the days of Mary Tudor (when my own house was built) there was built, also overlooking the seaport, the Hostellerie de Guillaume-le-Conquerant, where there is a legend that Mme de Sévigné passed by. At all events the Aga Khan and the Begum Aga Khan once called for me on my farm and drove me in their Rolls to eat lobster there. When I saw it again the place was closed and up for sale. Had there been a dearth of millionaires, princes and gourmets?

I have learned to beware of dreams—dreams of William the Conqueror's seaport, dreams engendered by that chocolate shop opposite the church where a master cook makes some of the finest home-made chocolates to be bought in France. The heart of Dives was pretty, but the outskirts were heavy with the smoke of factory chimneys, and there was a sullen discontent under a crust of beauty. The town hall is in the main highway and turns its back on the tax collector's office where one goes three times a year to pay one's income tax to help General de Gaulle balance his budget.

Patsy and Jacques Poirot were still tenants of Andrée's father, Dr Salmont, at 'Montauzan', former stables converted into a sort of hunting lodge, with a vast lawn, some Scots pines and a superb view over the low part of the village and the distant bay of Le Havre. The white gates of 'Montauzan' stood at right angles to those of 'Bois Lurette', the Pradeau estate, and both opened out on the roundabout where five roads met. The rue Pasteur led steeply down to the village, the Chemin de San Carlo bordered the former property of the Countess de Béarn, Cathedral Lane led to the 'Pelouses', the Bellay farm and the Michelins on the right and to the Levannier farm and to our own on the left. The road to St Vaast separated the Pradeau estate from 'Montauzan'. Finally, there was a narrow tortuous road with beautiful views that led to the cemetery and the station.

The two older Poirot boys were of university age. Anne was growing into a very pretty teenager with a particularly sweet disposition, while the youngest, Phillip, was still relatively little. Anybody might have thought that this admirable family who never quarrelled and all kept open house would by now consider itself complete. But Patsy, as gay as she was erudite, had a veritable genius for surprising her friends. A few days before Christmas she announced that she was adopting a little Indian girl of fourteen months who was about to arrive by air from New Delhi.

It can be imagined that this news, which ran round the village like wildfire, mightily intrigued the feminine population, myself included. Curiosity, jealousy, admiration, rubbed shoulders. We thought it high-minded of her to save a little child from starvation. We longed to see what it looked like. As it appeared to have no Christian name Patsy wrote a number of girls' names on a sheet of paper and handed this paper to her children, asking them to choose the one they thought most fitting for the new arrival. They went through the list carefully and crossed all of them out till they came to the name Karin.

Patsy arrived with Karin on New Year's Eve. The aeroplane

from New Delhi had landed in Paris just too late for the village to bring traditional gifts on Christmas Day to this much awaited child from the East, but it certainly made up for it afterwards. One took toys, another a cot, another a pram, another a baby park, another a dress—and so on until this dark-eyed pearl was surrounded by countless marks of fond attention.

Her history was, of course, bathed in romantic ignorance. We merely supposed that had she not in the first place been gathered up in merciful hands she would have died from starvation. Fate, which had allowed her to be rescued and flown over mountains and oceans to a land where she was going to be cherished, had also endowed her with a strange and fascinating beauty. We thought her as pretty and elegant as a princess. We talked to her in French. I absurdly wondered if she would respond more naturally to English. Her eyes rewarded me with rippling laughter.

Some weeks later Patsy, as if she had not surprised us enough already, came out with another piece of news. She and her husband had finally decided to buy a house of their own. Hitherto they had found it simpler to rent 'Montauzan', this amusing long, low house with its view through the Scots pines to the Channel. The youthful Andrée Pradeau and her family were, of course, excellent friends of the Poirots, and the children of both families bathed together and went to the same parties. But what an urge we all have, at one time or another, to own a dream house. Perhaps Annette Laurent, being so busy with her exciting new acquisition at Vauville, may have inspired Patsy to do the same. At all events, after searching everywhere in the neighbourhood they had, said Patsy, discovered the ideal place. They were going to buy the Bellay Farm!

This news was immensely intriguing. Quite apart from the fact that we were friends, it concerned all of us in the vicinity—the Pradeaus because they would lose a tenant but gain a neighbour, the Levanniers and ourselves because what happened to a farm so near us was of considerable import.

The next thing we heard was that the Poirots felt that ten acres of ground was too much for the sort of family house that they hoped to make of it. In this they were right. Ten acres was too small for a farm but too much for a family like Patsy's, which had no intention of owning a single cow. As Mme Bellay insisted on selling the whole in one piece, Patsy approached both

Andrée Pradeau and me with the suggestion that one of us might take a few acres of grassland and orchard off her hands.

The split-up had been worked out very roughly like this. The Poirots were willing to pay a certain price for the farmhouse, the outbuildings and the cider orchards on which these stood if they could find another buyer or buyers for the remainder of the Bellay estate. The land in question bordered Cathedral Lane on one side and the Chemin du Loup on the other. The Chemin du Loup separated the Bellay place from the Michelins', the Michelin house being exactly opposite that of the Levanniers'.

My own answer marked a total misunderstanding of the situation. I said that bearing in mind the normal value of farmland the price sounded uneconomic. The Pradeaus, I think, had different reasons for declining the offer. But these green acres did find purchasers at the price and very quickly. Each of them (there were two) said he would build a house on his share.

It was then that there very slowly began to dawn on me the existence of a town-planning scheme.

When the Pelouses found somebody willing to develop it, thatched cottages might turn it into a middle-class residential area. This was already happening at San Carlo, with cottages built on about a fifth of an acre of land. The Bellay land could also be built on, but under slightly different conditions.

Meanwhile the town-planners had apparently decided that when all the cottages were built in the development area, Cathedral Lane would prove too narrow, too leafy and too pretty for the motor-cars that would appear on the scene. It was therefore planned to enlarge it. Down would come the century-old trees which the squirrels so loved and which joined their boughs in the form of a celestial arch. Poor Andrée had some nightmares ahead! Patsy, however, felt that if she and her family took up residence at the Bellay farmhouse it would be nice to have so many neighbours. It was her theory that the neighbourhood would become the most fashionable of the village. We hoped she was right, but what a lot of noise and clutter, with bulldozers clawing up the earth and trees crashing down! The squirrels, the birds and the wild flowers would soon be gone.

The first warm days made me illogically happy. We lunched in the kitchen with the door wide open, and by midday, as if expecting us, the cows would all come to lie down as near to us as they could, for they loved our company and the sound of our voices. We would see them, perhaps twelve or fourteen, on the other side of the fence that separated the orchard from the daffodils and narcissi in the garden. Their serene content made us also feel content, almost as if nothing terrible could ever happen. Indeed, when one stood in the garden and looked across valleys and trees to the Louis XIII château on the farther hill, one realized that nothing could have changed much visually from the days of the French kings. The elegant château peeped out as it had always done from the thick wood which in April was carpeted with lilies-of-the-valley and orchids. There was not another roof in sight. The countryside miraculously had certain aspects of changelessness. This was what was so terribly dangerous about it. To the anger of many, this was what remained so picturesquely and healthily old-fashioned about it. It was this peace and serenity that was no longer so easy to find in other more highly industrialized countries.

I had already experienced this false sense of security in the early summer of 1940 when the flowers in this same garden had bloomed so peacefully, when the sun had shone so brightly, while only a few miles away at Rouen the German tanks were rolling over the bridges of the Seine on the eve of the French capitulation.

But of what was I now afraid? Of the bulldozers in the Countess of Béarn's once lovely park? Of the sound of crashing trees? Of the damage the young farmers were unwittingly inflicting on hedges, wild flowers and birds with their hormones and chemical sprays? Of the staggering prices that intelligent, charming friends seemed to consider it normal to have to pay for a modest country house?

Busy yourself with pruning your rose trees, picking your violets and planning tomorrow's lunch, I told myself. How stupidly fearful can a woman become!

The running of the house had become a comparatively automatic affair. The fact of having no servant, not even a daily, simplified matters rather than the contrary. As long as I remained physically able to do everything myself, including the washing and ironing of household linen which most young housewives would not be willing to undertake these days, the saving in wages and one's own equanimity is immense. One does at least remain mistress of one's own domain. My personal wants, with a house and wardrobe quite adequately stocked, had become, alas, small. Money was no longer able to buy the things I really wanted. Whenever I was in London I dreamed of the country. Now that I was too often in the country I sometimes hated it, and it was only on the rare occasions when I thought about the possibility of losing the house that I ever paid much attention to possessing it.

Though we were in no way circumscribed to a maximum budget, I deliberately ran my small kingdom for the equivalent of twenty pounds a week, which sum included regular deliveries of corn for the hens and Russian anthracite (it was not possible to obtain Cardiff) at twenty-seven pounds a ton for the Aga and our central heating. I took a pride in running the place on the smallest effective budget, proud to be emulating the head of state who never allowed his ministers to run a budget deficit! France alone seemed capable of balancing her budget. We may both have been too scrupulous. Those who are careful with money are apt to criticize those who are less so—and that, human frailty being what it is, can lead to a backlash.

Now that we were on top of Easter it was lovely to think that sunshine and golden hours on the beach must surely soon be with us. Nearly all the summer residents arrived in our village for the Easter week-end. They came to see that all was well in villas that had been closed all winter. They brought news of what had been happening in Paris, and we told them of the small insignificant things that had made our small talk.

Old Dr Durville and his wife had arrived as usual at their beautiful villa with its splendid lawn and the fig tree that every August pushed its luscious fruit through their bedroom window, thus providing the Spartan doctor with an agreeable breakfast. Mme Durville was a particular friend. She and her husband had brought with them the pekinese who would so cruelly remind me of the one I had lost the previous winter. My husband had bought Lin Tin for Mme Durville in London and arranged for the puppy to come to her by air. Lin Tin had become the most beloved of pekinese and I must go and call on the Durvilles and take Mme Durville a big bunch of sweet scented violets from my garden. Tomorrow would be Easter Day.

First I would buy the papers and collect the mail.

It was at this point that I heard about the existence at the town hall of a blueprint or map to show exactly how the new highway would by-pass the village.

M. Salesse, whom my husband and I had met coming down the stairs and to whom one of us had turned for information, now said:

'Yes, indeed, there is a map, all very official and up to date. I expect the town clerk has it in his office. Shall we go and see?'

We followed him into the town clerk's office.

'I'm rather busy just now,' said the town clerk. 'Wouldn't Monday do for the map?'

'Oh no!' I broke in. 'Not Monday! I couldn't spend the whole of Easter in uncertainty. Please let us see it now!'

The look of sudden understanding that came over the features of the town clerk should have warned me that all the notables of the village must by now have been aware of our predicament, which they had doubtless discussed at length, surprised that we should remain the last to be informed. Opening a wide drawer, the civic dignitary produced a voluminous rolled-up parchment which he handed to M. Salesse, saying:

'Let me have it back soon. I'm supposed to keep it locked up.'

M. Salesse took it gingerly. The room was crowded.

'Where can we inspect it?' I whispered.

'Upstairs in the library, I think. We need plenty of space to spread it out.'

In the quiet of the library, under the light of the tall windows, he unrolled the map and laid it out on the polished table, placing a book at each corner to keep it flat. Then tracing the course of the road with his index finger, he said:

'The by-pass, coming from the direction of Touques, enters the map here, not far from the stream that waters the orchard below my house. Are you with me?'

'Not quite,' I said. 'Let me get my bearings first. Is this "Bois Lurette"?'

'That's right.'

'And this is the road to St Vaast?'

'Right again. You will notice that the by-pass cuts the road to St Vaast at right angles, then climbs straight as an arrow across your home orchard, past your white entrance gates, past those newly planted walnut trees, then right through the heart of your island site (the one you call the Pointe) until it runs right off this map to join the Deauville–Caen highway.'

'Right through my home orchard!' I echoed, dazed, my fear paralysing me. 'What's this small square in the middle of my orchard which the road seems to pass right over?'

'That?' said M. Salesse. 'Why, that's your house!'

# 2

I SHALL not pretend that I took the news stoically. The implications were too grave.

The desire to own a house, a piece of ground and a cow is probably inherent in most women who are apt to cling to what appears safe and permanent. I may not, of course, have been wise to choose this particular part of the world to start a dynasty. However, in spite of the mud, the long winters and the lack of sunshine, the house itself was snug and, with all my small possessions within its walls, I had reason to love it. Though we had only owned it for thirty years, we had lost it and regained it, though pillaged, and had been obliged to refurnish it altogether with scarcely a penny to do so in 1946. We then watched it grow again, with my mother and my son enjoying spells of happiness together. My mother had died in the room that was now my own. My husband and I supposed that one day our son and daughter-in-law, the excitement of their travels over, would inherit it and perhaps, who could tell, there would be another century to add to the four it had already seen. A fragment of myself, oh, a very tiny one, might remain in it.

M. Salesse in the town hall, trying to make things better, had said:

'If it comes to the worst they'll pay you for expropriation, you know.'

I saw what remained of my earthly treasures being dumped in the garden, and silently I exclaimed: 'Oh no, not twice in a lifetime!' In 1940 we had fled leaving absolutely everything behind, with the lunch laid on the kitchen table. Six years later not a stitch of my clothing, not anything that as a young married woman I had loved and treasured did I get back. I refurnished the house with what I could carry by hand from England on long, dangerous journeys, or with what I could send in parcels to my mother. But on this still unknown date in the future the problem in reverse seemed even more terrifying. What would I do with the contents of the house when somebody came to tell me that my home was being expropriated? Would I have to lug every single picture back to England under my arm, as I had brought them?

The sound of bulldozers in my brain prevented me from sleeping that night, and indeed for many nights thereafter. But I refused to talk about the matter to anybody. Not once did I broach the subject. Yet all the notables must have known and they were probably laughing at us behind our backs. Old Maître Vincent, the notary, meeting me some weeks later in the village main street, was obviously itching to say something. He had negotiated the sale of the farm to us in those far-off pre-war days. I had a special respect for him because he was, in these days of latent Communism, a sincere patriot. As a young soldier he had fought in the hell of Verdun. During the Second World War he had lost his wife and two of his children during the bombardments of Caen. The house in which they were living disappeared and they with it. No trace of them was ever found.

He said: 'Things are difficult in England, I fear, what with the devaluation of sterling and the political situation.' Then with a smile: 'But I have no doubt that things will right themselves. England always wins the last battle. By the way, that new by-pass is scheduled to go right through your house. But not just yet, oh no, not just yet. After I'm dead, maybe. But the plan still holds. I expect you'll be summoned to a meeting. They'll listen to any objections you may care to make. Not that they'll act on them. But they'll listen. However, don't worry. It's not just yet.'

'Supposing I wished to sell?'

The old notary smiled the way he did when he needed to explain patiently a detail of law.

'No, no,' he said, 'you couldn't sell with a thing like that hanging over the house. Not at any price worth taking. But as I say, don't worry. It's not going to happen just yet.'

Maître Vincent had answered a question my husband and I had hardly dared formulate. If we could not leave the house to our son, might we not take a dislike to it? Might we feel a terrible necessity to get rid of it before the bulldozers thundered across the orchard, tearing down our apple trees. Would it not be wiser to sell the place and get out? Might it not be a case of 'if thine eye offend thee, pluck it out!' The notary had answered this question in a voice that still mocked my ears: 'No, no, you couldn't sell with a thing like that hanging over the house.' But being after all a man of law and preciseness, had he not added: '. . . not at any price worth taking.'

But I knew, of course, that unless I was driven to it, I would not abandon the house. To do that would be tantamount to deserting a friend in trouble.

A small plaque in stainless steel was let into the fireplace of our low room. Engraved by a London artisan whose workrooms I had discovered under the roofs and crazy chimney pots of a tall building in New Bond Street, it reflected on winter evenings the flames of the four-feet logs. My husband and I at that time were in the full flood of our activities. I had felt a strange desire to mark the house with our fleeting tenancy, for what were so few years amongst so many?

*1555–1955*

*We thank thee dear God, for having spared this house through four centuries.*

*The Robert Henrey family*
*Easter 1955*

*Normandie herbagère, éclatante et mouillée*
*Nous voulons venir vivre un jour, doux et vieillis*
*Parmi tes près, au fond d'une maison rayée*
*Lucie Delarue-Mardrus.*

After a while I began to feel less bitter. The unhappiness was still there, but I tried to ward it off by threats. If the roof caved in, I told myself, I would not even have it repaired. How stupid I had been to have the front of the house repainted! And why had I planted that blue cedar? I should not plant another tree. The only person I could trust myself to talk things over with was Andrée Pradeau, gentle, intelligent and wise, in whom I found qualities I admired so much in my own sex.

I never went to 'Bois Lurette' without having the strange impression of stepping into a fairy-tale. The forest trees, and the little bulbous spire and porcelain crosses surmounting the curiously shaped roof with its weather-beaten russet-coloured tiles, gave it a mysterious, Russian atmosphere. The green paint of the façade flaked off into the flower beds at the base of the low privet hedge. The entrance was enticing with the white lacy curtains gathered by feminine ribbons behind the glass panels. Outside, lanterns creaked in the wind, and in front of all the windows there were little wooden balconies from which one could almost touch the overhanging boughs of the trees.

In the rotunda, with its own pointed red-tiled roof and strong northern light streaming in through wide windows from the direction of the English coast, Claude Monet, Pierre Bonnard and Edouard Vuillard painted pictures of immortal beauty. Their canvases which now fetch such undreamt-of fortunes were, while being painted, put away at night in those built-in receptacles under the windows, each having a grooved side to hold it in place and prevent it from rubbing against its neighbour. In special drawers and boxes, still daubed with their colours, they kept their brushes and paints. You can finger all this now, calling back the genius of another age.

'Bois Lurette' was then owned by the Bernheims. The brothers Josse and Gaston, both born in 1870, married two sisters who were painted by Vuillard seated on the terrace of 'Bois Lurette'. Gaston Bernheim, himself a painter, who once had a model who was posing for Derain, took the name of Gaston de Villers. The Bernheims used to drive round the countryside in an early six-cylinder Delaunay-Belleville with a coloured chauffeur. Josse Bernheim's two sons, Henry and Jean Dauberville, now write enchanting books about the Impressionists and the many people like Roussel, Sacha Guitry and Charlotte Lysès who were guests of their father, their uncle or of themselves at 'Bois Lurette' till it was sold in 1932. The artist Raoul Dufy incidentally spent every summer there from 1920 till 1932. He loved to paint the pier at Trouville and regattas at Deauville.

Andrée was preparing the house for the wedding of her daughter Danièle in late June. As soon as she arrived from Paris with her husband at week-ends she changed into jeans and sneakers and redecorated the house. Laurence, another daughter, slim, almost boyish, with features of great beauty, helped hang hessian of gay designs on the walls to give a tapestry effect.

To see Andrée in jeans with flecks of white paint in her fair hair was proof of the many things she turned her hand to. She also kept the accounts of the farm, supervised the meals, ran the house and found time (she was an exquisite needlewoman) to make curtains. The house was immense. On the second floor was her workroom, papered with white and blue flowers against a grey background. The paper was peeling off in parts, and maps and blueprints were fastened by drawing-pins to the wall. A map of the estate, for instance, showed the ancient rights over every hedge.

There were two plain white deal cupboards side by side, each six feet wide and two feet deep. These dated from the Bernheim days and had obviously proved irresistible, because of the smooth width of their surfaces, to guests who either ran short of canvases or just could not resist daubing everything within sight with paint. The closed doors of the cupboard on the left had been treated with light blue wash, and then used as a full canvas; the doors of the one on the right were treated with light pink wash and used for four separate scenes, one on each panel. Who, in a house full of famous Impressionists, painted these enchanting scenes? Gaston Bernheim and his guests must have shared the fun. The larger is a view of the great lawn bordered by forest trees and having the bay of Le Havre in the distance.

This is what Claude Monet would have seen from the windows of the rotunda, but it would also have been the view that Gaston Bernheim would have had from the terrace of his upstairs bedroom. The other scenes are a constant puzzle to Andrée as she sews or irons. As half a century must have passed since they were done, trees have grown or been cut down, walks have altered. Andrée said she thought that one of the panels represented a view of the Mount Canisy, others favourite nooks and vantage points in the grounds of the estate. Did Claude Monet, Bonnard or Vuillard ever come up with Gaston de Villers on a rainy afternoon and join in this romp? Later Henry Dauberville, writing from Paris, asked me to come and see the famous picture representing his mother and his aunt on 'La Terrasse de Bois Lurette' by Ed Vuillard. He added: 'I would need pages and pages to tell you about all the famous people who were guests of my father and uncle at "Bois Lurette"—Claude Monet lived there, so did Bonnard. Georges Feydeau and Octave Mirbeau stayed there. Now I'm off to Venice, but come and see me later. As for the old cupboards, I expect my Uncle Gaston de Villers was responsible!'

Andrée, I think, treats these masterpieces of anonymous paternity as they deserve. She had stacked two kitchen chairs on top of one of the cupboards with their backs hanging down against the tops of the paintings. I said to her: 'Supposing they really are by Claude Monet? Or even by Raoul Dufy, who so liked painting sailing boats at Deauville?' Having excited her interest we discovered some more pictures on the sides—a seaside study with a very French-looking tent on the sands and a sailing boat on the sea. 'There!' I cried. 'Couldn't that be Dufy?'

But Andrée knew that what was really on my mind was the road. She would ask her husband to make inquiries. She hated to see me miserable, and, though she tried to console me by pointing out that the road was also scheduled to pass over one of their own orchards on the other side of the road to St Vaast, she knew it was not quite so bad. Her house, the trees, the meadows, the greenhouses, the farm and the lawns where their sheep grazed under the chestnut trees would presumably remain for quite a time yet as an island of beauty in a sea of trouble. Nevertheless in answer to her proffered help I said: 'Yes, if you could do that,' but I guessed in advance what the reply would be. However, it was doing me good to talk about it, and then (we were still in her workroom) I saw near the window a photograph of her father, Dr Salmont, who now owned 'Bois Lurette', in the uniform of a French army doctor during the First World War.

'Oh,' I exclaimed, 'what a round, chubby, youthful face! He's the image of Bernard, your youngest boy.'

She laughed and looked at the photograph with new interest. 'Do you think so, really? My father went through Verdun, the Chemin des Dames, all the cruellest infernos of that intolerable war of mud and trenches. Only a few men of his regiment survived.'

He had married an American girl from a small town near Pittsburg, Pennsylvania, and there had been two children, Andrée and a son who had been killed while taking part in the French Resistance Movement during the Second World War. Andrée had just shown me the beautiful corner bedroom on the other side of the corridor which had been his. I think that, like her mother, she still saw him everywhere. Truly it had been a case of 'Those whom the gods love best . . .' Her father was now old and, being a doctor, had no illusions about the seriousness of an illness that had struck him some months earlier. He couldn't bear to be parted from Andrée's mother for the briefest moment. I had learnt to love both of them during a holiday which they had spent with Andrée and her husband the previous summer, and since there was nothing that the doctor enjoyed so much as a freshly boiled egg, I took a delight in bringing him the very best and freshest from my own poultry.

Andrée's mother now lived between her sick husband and the memory of her beloved son. Sometimes, when a yearning for America took hold of her, she caught herself asking (in spite of her love for her husband) whether she had been right as a young bride to expatriate herself to a country whose politics and ambitions had suddenly become so cruelly and stupidly opposed to those of her own. But though there were clearly moments when this worried and puzzled her, the atmosphere being so different from that of her youth, her thoughts invariably reverted to her son. As I had met him and could talk about him she felt a rather special affection for me.

Andrée and I were passing down the corridor. 'Tell me about your mother?'

'I telephoned her just before I left Paris,' she said. 'Her voice alarmed me and I said: "Mother is there something wrong?" My mother answered: "He is asleep, so I think and I think, and I am sad!"'

At the top of the stairs Andrée opened a door to peep into the bedroom of her daughter Laurence. Laurence had an Irish Setter, Loïca, who, like Mary's little lamb, went wherever she did, sleeping under Laurence's bed and guarding her so ferociously that even Andrée had learned to be careful before entering her daughter's room.

But the room was empty. The animal, who with her young mistress had lunched with us only a couple of days earlier, was now probably with Laurence at the potting sheds. The bedroom with its adjoining dressing-room had immensely wide french windows that from this height afforded breathtaking views across country—but a countryside that because of the forest trees in the foreground appeared much wilder than I had expected. A giant

Thuja, for instance, of perfect pyramidical shape, gave the scene a Wagnerian quality and made me realize why Laurence was so deeply attached to the place. I found myself hoping fervently that the new road would never rob this place of its romantic link with a quietness and a wildness that cheap cottages and handkerchief-sized lawns so effectively destroyed.

# THE 'REVOLUTION' OF MAY

# 3

SOMETHING was happening in the climate of the land that was both disturbing and difficult to analyse. In a nearby village Mme de L. was feeding a dish of tea to her little dog in the drawing-room of her villa where the daffodils I had brought her from our garden made a splash of gold. She said almost plaintively, with one eye still on her little dog happily lapping up the tea: 'You know, my dear, we finally bought a small bar of gold.' Her husband, the aged philosopher, began telling us about a forebear who in some other crisis in France's troubled economic history had also thought it wise to buy gold bars. He had them in a little black bag which he carried about with him everywhere, but one day on arrival at a railway terminus a porter stacking his other luggage on a trolley spied the little black bag and picked that up too. Then off he went by an exit reserved for porters wheeling luggage to the station forecourt in search of a cab. The owner of the gold, it appears, noticing that his little black bag had disappeared, almost died of shock, and when at last he retrieved it, decided that it would be better to sell his gold for the sake of his peace of mind. 'Which', said the philosopher, 'he did!'

I refrained from asking Mme de L. if she also carried her bar of gold around with her. 'You don't think it was a good idea, buying a little gold?' she asked with a touchingly innocent smile. I said I really didn't know, but at least it was less heavy to walk about with than an acre of land, and it remained legal to own it. At this point I checked myself. Land also was legal to own, but what happened when somebody else felt like grabbing it?

Fanned by nightly propaganda on the state-owned television, the whole village was slowly becoming educated to the magic properties of gold, as also to the wickedness of the Americans, the improvidence of the British, and the importance of keeping a nation with a greater industrial potential temporarily out of the Common Market. There was, of course, a great feeling of national satisfaction in the air. A few people might have bought some of the golden Napoleons, so warm to the touch, that could be purchased with admirable anonymity at any bank, but most of them played the *tiercé* (the first three horses to pass the winning post in a race) as people in Britain did the pools. To back them in their right order brings fabulous odds; in what is known as 'disorder' rather less. The shopkeepers sweetly commiserated with me about all those unpleasant things that were happening to the pound, but this also helped to make them feel good. London, with its long-haired youths and girls in mini-skirts, much featured on television, seemed morally a dangerous place. All these considerations, however, were as nothing compared with the heartbreak of parents and children before the latter were required to sit for the *baccalauréat*. This school-leaving examination was wrecking the peace of an entire nation which, but for such a headache, was otherwise enjoying the giddy excitement of riding the crest of a wave. For the parents the *baccalauréat* was a matter of retaining a status symbol. For the children it was a matter of earning the smiles of their parents and a breathing-space before the next confrontation with the complications of growing up. The next stage, though they would continue to be sheltered from the outside world, would be academically tougher. The first bout of idleness, the first grave error, and they would be cast out like the chaff from a gigantic, scholastic threshing-machine. But the prizes were great. Even Brigitte, our dear Brigitte, was simply longing to become a teacher. Georgette was very proud of her.

In front of our well with its thatched pointed roof was a patch of unsightly stinging nettles and, as I refused to allow hormone spraying, I set about pulling them up, roots and all, with gloved hands.

This exercise calls for patience. Stinging nettles hide an inch or more under the grass a complicated network of thick yellow cables, and, unless these are dragged out and burnt, nothing worth while is accomplished. Though not yet in flower, the nettles all about me were nearly as tall as I am. To be tall is one of my secret wishes, one of those tall willowy women on whom clothes hang so elegantly. However, I am what I am and I attack these nettles with vigour, aware that every one of them is a redoubtable enemy capable of giving me an uncomfortable rash. I am surprised at my own tenacity, for I have already spent several hours at this task which nobody else would dream of undertaking, but I manage to convince myself that this sort of work is really useful, more useful than the feminine nothings that occupy so much of my time, knitting, sewing, hanging linen up on the line, not to mention my passion for solving crossword puzzles and looking up uncommon words in the dictionary.

The thatched roof over my well is shaped like the hats Vietnamese women wear. The straw was once elegant and blond. Now it has become thin with age, and not only with age because good thatching will last a lifetime, but with ill treatment by certain cows that cannot resist the temptation to reach up their long, powerful necks and tug with all their might at the loose straw. When in exasperation I complain to Jacques Déliquaire, my farmer, he exclaims, with a smile on his red, weather-beaten but youthful face: 'Heavens, ma'am, a fine cow is a tall beast!'

My conviction that work done in the open air is more meritorious than a great deal of what one is apt to do indoors is a left-over from girlhood. Our schoolmistress had a favourite dictation which made a deep impression on me. It concerned two neighbours each of whom had a house, a wife and a few acres of land. The lazy man was always putting off till tomorrow what he ought to have been doing today, while the diligent man went quietly about his business, sowing, reaping, haymaking all at the right time. 'I'll start cutting the hay tomorrow,' said the lazy man. 'I merely need to work twice as fast as my neighbour and I'll soon catch up with him.' The next morning the sun shone and it was an ideal day for haymaking, but the lazy man was invited to a wedding and off he went to feast and dance. On the morrow it rained and as he had caught cold in the barn where they supped and danced he stayed in bed. I need scarcely add that this went on and on until the lazy man came to a deplorable end. That was the object of the tale. Our mistress considered (and so did the textbook) that no subject for a little girl's dictation had any merit unless it had a moral. My mother's influence was doubtless even more responsible for that feeling ingrained in me that a woman especially should never—outdoors or indoors—be seen idle, but the tales read in girlhood do stick to one through life. Marcia Davenport says in her personal record that the reading of Grimm's fairy-tales with their cruelty and fantasy were probably in part responsible for her own gift of story-telling, though she also had the good fortune to benefit from a prolonged little-girl closeness to the grown-up world of a remarkable mother. Freak childhoods and excessive reading are becoming lamentably rare. Perhaps we would have less unhappiness in the universities if the aridity of modern scientific education had been prefaced by childhood flights of imagination into the worlds of magic and wonder, the gods and goddesses of Greek and Roman times, the *Arabian Nights* and fairy-tales of Grimm, the deeds of Norsemen and the haunting myths of the *Götterdämmerung*, all frowned on by modern left-wing teachers and parents alike.

Once a patch of soil had been cleared of nettles, it revealed itself dark and rich, and I planned to take some of this to the front garden to put on the rose beds. My wheelbarrow was nearly full when I saw a light delivery van coming down the drive. A few moments later a good-looking young man got out, opened the doors at the back and carefully deposited on the grass a shining white washing-machine.

'Oh no,' I exclaimed petulantly, supposing him to be an itinerant salesman, 'not that. If I had wanted one I would have bought one long ago, but I prefer, believe it or not, to save my money and wash the linen by hand the old-fashioned way.'

This statement didn't appear to rile him a bit. Puzzled, but giving me the nicest professional smile, he asked:

'You are Mme Déliquaire, aren't you?'

This unexpected approach changed everything.

'Alas, no,' I answered. 'Mme Jacques Déliquaire is my farmer's wife.'

'Where can I find her?'

'At the farm presumably. Drive back to the white gates, turn to the left and the farm is about a quarter of a mile farther on. You will see it on your right.'

Losing interest in me he lifted his washing-machine back into the van. The smile had gone from his face, and I think he must have been shaken by my appearance and my muddy jeans. Jumping back into the driving seat he was about to switch on when he suddenly had an idea.

'Would you like a prospectus? Just in case?'

'Does it describe the one you're taking to Mme Déliquaire?'

'Absolutely. There's a picture with instructions and the price.'

This was tempting Eve under the apple trees of her own garden. What woman could resist such proferred information about what a neighbour, one's own farmer's wife, was doing?

'Well,' I said, squaring my conscience with the thought that it was the man pushing the information into my hands, not I asking for it. 'Well,' I repeated, 'if you want me to?'

'Look!' he said, pointing to the picture. 'A real beauty. If one day you think you can afford it, remember—ten per cent down, the rest in instalments. O.K.?'

'O.K.,' I said.

As he disappeared up the orchard I turned to my wheelbarrow, piling earth in but with less peace of mind. Was I feeling the way Eve had felt after biting into the apple?

In fact the next day it all passed off very well because, when Georgette arrived with the milk, it was she who exclaimed: 'I don't need to tell you that I've got a washing-machine!'

'The delivery van came here by mistake. The young man must have told you. I hope you don't mind my knowing.'

'Of course, not in the slightest,' she said, laughing. 'As a matter of fact I gave Jacques a sort of ultimatum. If I am to go on helping him in the orchards and with the animals, then he must bring more domestic appliances into the home. That's fair, isn't it? I just hadn't the strength to go on washing all his things and ours by hand. If it were merely a case of Brigitte's things and mine, that would be different. But a man's things are too hard. So he agreed. He said I could have my washing-machine, and now that I've got it I'm delighted. You must come and see it working.'

'I will,' I promised, 'and I don't blame you for insisting. Jacques was probably very flattered that you asked him. I suppose I'm merely being obstinate not having one myself, but I hate the idea of becoming a slave to mechanical things that can so easily go wrong. Besides, I wash often but in small quantities. My problem is different from yours. By the way how is Monsieur Paul?'

Monsieur Paul had been unwell. He was a sort of uncle by adoption, an intimate friend of the whole family. Rosalie, Georgette's Ukrainian-born mother, kept a specially friendly eye on him, it being her opinion that men without wives were to be pitied. Especially bachelors. I am not sure how Monsieur Paul first arrived in the village, but in his younger days he had been a gentlemen's hairdresser and barber, a status which ever afterwards had endowed him with the title of 'monsieur'. At one time, Georgette informed me, he had taken rooms with a widow, but the widow died and her children, anxious to lay hands on their inheritance, the house and all the furniture in it, gave summary notice to her lodger, taking his scant belongings and making a pile of them in the garden. There followed a rather sad period for Monsieur Paul during which he was reduced to playing dominoes with other retired gentlemen in the local cafés. Then suddenly he found himself a super job!

Not all the hotels in the village had, like the Bellevue, become holiday houses for employees of a state monopoly. One of the nicest, overlooking the Syndicat d'Initiative and the *plage*, had been bought by an astute developer who had turned it into flats or studios where people of relatively modest means, to whom camping sites were anathema, could have a summer place all of their own by the sea. Every so often in front of the main entrance a motor-coach would unload its cargo of prospective purchasers from Paris or elsewhere. Then out from his office to welcome these charming people and to show them round would come the representative of the owner—none other than Monsieur Paul!

Sometimes, after their business was over, whether to their satisfaction or not one couldn't tell, and having an hour or more to waste before their motor-coach took them back to Paris or to whatever other city they belonged, the tired travellers would wander through the narrow and rather deserted streets of our village (out of season) wondering whether they would like it or not. Some of them gave one the impression that they must already be retired. Others were doubtless looking forward apprehensively to the day when their colleagues would arrange an office party so that they could be presented with the appropriate leaving gift. Nearly all had the tired look of people who had worked long hours for small reward, and as the men paced slowly along, their knotty hands clasped behind their backs and as the women clustered together in Sunday-best clothes and shoes that pinched, one was tempted to speculate on the questionable allurements of a period when they would have too much idle time on their hands. Would this village give them what they had dreamed about all through their working lives? The beach used to be a children's beach. Deauville was for the millionaires, the actresses, the lovely models, the writers and the painters. Cabourg was famous for its casino. But this was for the children whose nannies sat gossiping under multicoloured tents, knowing that their charges could come to no harm on the soft expanses of golden sand. Soon perhaps it would become the seaside resort of the retireds at sixty. But of course for Monsieur Paul, with his new functions, his new responsibilities, it was the future, the exciting tomorrow with its lucrative horizon.

Monsieur Paul had a light motor-cycle and mounted on this he would swiftly traverse the village on business and pleasure. By coincidence Georgette's mother Rosalie owned a machine of similar design on which this child of the vast Russian wheat plains, now looking exactly like a Russian peasant, travelled far afield to burn up her immense, never-flagging energy. One would meet her at the fair at Dozulé. 'Rosalie, what on earth are you doing here?' 'I've come to buy a dozen baby ducks,' she would say.

In winter I used to see Monsieur Paul in his black overcoat and round hat travelling at speed between his office and the place beyond the railway station where he lunched. Along the station road, bordered by plane trees which was also the road to the cemetery, blind Mr Schwartz would walk also on his way to lunch, tapping his white blind man's stick and holding the arm of the girl who acted as salesgirl in the little wool shop he owned in the village.

'By the way, how is Monsieur Paul?' I had asked Georgette.

'He should take a rest,' said Georgette. 'Fancy at his age going up and down all those stairs showing prospective customers round! What can you do? They do so like him. He inspires confidence! I must say that it's very pleasant to see him so interested in his work.'

'Rosalie says that Monsieur Paul is losing his fine appetite,' I said, 'I came upon her yesterday in the market-place in front of Mme Lemercier's stall. 'I fancy she feels he ought to be spoilt a little, but she told us that with the season about to start, her cottage to look after and Brigitte's coming First Communion she expects to be pretty busy during the next few weeks.'

In fact Rosalie had said: 'What with *my* season about to start...'
At Easter and in summer she looked after the villas of a number
of summer residents. She managed to put money away as only
women of her race and calibre knew how to, but, far from being
mean, she was always spoiling her daughter and her grand-
daughter. But she owned the house she lived in, a pretty house
with a fine garden on the outskirts of the village beyond the
railway line, and for the last twenty-five years, ever since her
husband died, she had regularly invested her war widow's
pension—with the interest thereon. Yes, with the interest, so
that it had already grown into a very tidy fortune. Besides this,
she sold her eggs and an occasional fowl, and the summer residents she worked for thought the world of her. As well they
might, because her capacity for hard work was without limit.
Brigitte's First Communion was her present chief preoccupation.
A girl's First Communion was still considered the biggest single
event in family life. Her wedding, of course, was very solemn,
very wonderful, very important, but it did not necessarily take
place at home. For the girl it was the end of one form of life, the
start of another. But her First Communion was an immensely
important family affair which in the old days in the depth of the
country amongst farming people took place on the farm, with
feasting and merriment lasting some three days and nights. This is
precisely what Georgette and Jacques Déliquaire planned for
Brigitte, then approaching her thirteenth year. They were cutting
the wood to build the great tent that would jut out from one of
their barns, and the lambs that were grazing on my piece of land
called the Pointe were destined for the rejoicings, as indeed were
all those fat geese and ducks and those noisy, screeching, cackling
guinea-fowl that kept invading my home orchard and flying
into the kitchen garden. This contrast between the countrified
scenes of the past and the revolutionary rumblings now tearing
at the very structure of society was perhaps what puzzled and
misled one most. Once again it seemed like sunshine in a summer
garden whilst the first German tanks crossed the bridges over the
Seine at Rouen and the oil refineries at Le Havre were ferociously
burning, spelling anguish and defeat. Which was true? The
sun and the flowers or the desolation?

Said Rosalie to the women in front of Mme Lemercier's stall:
'I'm going to give Brigitte, my grand-daughter, a gold wrist-

watch for her First Communion. A pure gold wrist-watch—all in pure gold.'

Out had come this magic word, twice repeated to ensure that we had understood the meaning of it. Now, sure of the full attention of her audience, Rosalie went on:

'Some people have blamed me for wanting to spend so much money on a little girl, a little girl of twelve and a half, but that little girl is my grand-daughter, and that is what she wants! She would like it to be a very small watch, though I am told that the smaller they are the more expensive they are likely to be. Now I will tell you a secret. We are going to buy the wrist-watch in Paris. Don't tell the local watchmaker. I don't want to hurt his feelings, but Paris is Paris and my son-in-law knows a watch-maker there who will sell it to us at cost price.'

'So you will all be going to Paris?'

'*They* are going to Paris,' she corrected with special emphasis on the 'they' to have us understand that 'they' signified Jacques and Georgette. 'They are going to Paris to buy a new suit for Jacques to wear at the ceremony, and an *ensemble* for my daughter, an elegant *ensemble* and a hat! Oh, my!' she said. 'Oh, my! If only I could describe to you all the gold neckchains and all the gold medallions that Brigitte has already received for the First Communion you would be astonished. I even wonder if she isn't being given too many lovely things. Jacques's widowed mother is giving her an electric record-player. The poor old lady has no idea what a record-player looks like, but that is what Brigitte asked for and so they will make a special expedition to Trouville, or perhaps even to Caen, to choose it.'

Madeleine Déliquaire, whose husband had been my tenant farmer when we came back to the village after the war, was now permanently in charge of a very fine villa in the rue Pasteur which leads down to the village from 'Bois Lurette'.

Leaving Rosalie still gossiping in front of Mme Lemercier's stall I went to see if Mme Quettel had an early lettuce. She had a small market garden in the low ground down by the sea and her produce was exceptionally good. I was just asking her if things were coming along in her garden as she hoped when once again Rosalie made her appearance.

'I have ordered a white hydrangea for Brigitte's First Communion!' she announced. 'They are less expensive if you place the order early.' Happy to extend the enumeration of everything that was being prepared for the festivities, she went on: 'When the "children" (Jacques and Georgette) went to visit my married sister at Le Creusot some time ago they drove through Rheims where they bought a case of champagne. When they got home, they hid it in a safe place so as not to be tempted to open it. So that will come in handy at the feast, though of course there will be plenty of other wines, special ones for every course.'

After bidding Mme Quettel good day, Rosalie and I had walked away from her stall together. Relapsing into her favourite Ukrainian pidgin French, she said to me confidentially with a twinkle:

'I heard you asking her how her flowers grow. Not likely she answer you. She too afraid you grow same flowers!'

At this point we parted for the day, each to our own business.

The following Sunday another of Georgette's visitors mistook my home orchard for hers. This is not a thing that happens often, but just then Berlequet was being transformed into a place worthy to receive its guests. On this occasion the visitor was a woman driving a small Citroën. I had taken my transistor out into the garden, intending to lighten the boredom of pulling up weeds while listening to the B.B.C.'s Sunday afternoon play, when the woman asked me the same question as the delivery man had done: 'Are you Mme Déliquaire?' So Georgette took it upon herself to explain everything when next she called with the milk. I had said to her:

'I hope you were at home when your visitor called on Sunday?'

'Yes, I was,' answered Georgette. 'I was expecting her, but as she was coming from Lisieux, and I knew the roads would be pretty crowded on a Sunday afternoon, I was a bit nervous.'

There was a pause. Then said Georgette:

'She's my cook!'

I must have looked surprised, because Georgette drew herself up and repeated with dignity:

'Yes, she's my cook, the cook I am engaging for three days to cook the meals during the festivities that follow Brigitte's First Communion. She will bring all the kitchen utensils with her, the dishes, the plates, the cutlery, the silver, the glassware and the linen. All the members of Jacques's family as well as of mine, even those who live farthest away, all of them, grown-ups and

children, have been invited. There will even be a friend of
Jacques's with whom he did his military service in Indo-China.
Doing things on such a big scale on the farm will obviously cost a
great deal of money, but for years past I have been putting
money aside for my daughter's First Communion. I want it to be
something that I shall remember all the rest of my life, and that
Brigitte herself will never, never forget. I was robbed of such an
experience for myself. My father had been killed and we were
living under the German occupation. My First Communion was
therefore a sad, lonely affair. I swore that if ever I had a daughter,
and could afford it, I would give her what I had dreamed of
having myself—all and even more. Her wedding? I can't be
certain of seeing it. The future is a riddle, and for a girl of only
twelve and a half her wedding still lies far ahead. But this First
Communion is now! So near that I can almost stretch an arm out
and feel it! Nobody can take that away from me!'

Georgette's voice had taken on an air of defiance. She was
afraid that I might blame her for the expense she was incurring.
She already sensed that I had been appalled at the cost of the
washing-machine which, like so many things in France, cost
infinitely more than their counterparts in England.

Nevertheless her tone soon softened. We both enjoyed these
moments of gossip, and it was only when I had done something
unwittingly to offend her that she sought to avoid them. To reach
the kitchen door she had to pass the garden gate and walk for a
few yards along a gravel path. The garden gate had an Austrian
cowbell tied to it, a lovely sounding bell I had brought back from
the Tyrol when my son was making his film there, and it gave me
warning of any stranger coming by. Even the cats when they
jumped over the gate were never so silent that they did not make
it tinkle, and as my hearing is as acute as an owl's I felt safer at
night. But when there had been some minor misunderstanding
over the farm, or what the cows had done to the young fruit trees,
Georgette came to my kitchen door so silently that to my infinite
regret I occasionally missed her. Thus she punished me. But now
she was happy and her tone was soft.

'Our parish priest', she said, 'is very pleased with Brigitte!
Not once has she ever been late for catechism.'

Her words were not without significance. In this ancient
province where medieval churches still abounded, jewels hidden

amongst the trees, most of them in remote villages were without priests or congregation. The strict banning of religious education in state schools, often the inspired agnosticism of left-wing teachers, contributed to a growing sense of frustration among children who tended to grow up without contentment, hope or patriotism. Only the sterile law of examination, followed by the success of the few and the elimination of the many, was inculcated. Fortunately Brigitte, as Georgette had said, was a model pupil at catechism, and our village priest, an affable and enlightened man, was pleased with her. Was she an exception? Were her broadminded parents exceptions? Who could truly judge? At all events the manner in which all three of them approached the religious side of the ceremony, the only important one, would happily make what was to follow—the feasting, the drinking, the singing, the practical jokes—a Christian, not a pagan occasion.

'It stands to reason,' said Georgette suddenly, and in just the right voice for what she was about to say. 'It stands to reason that you and your husband will be invited.'

I had not at all taken for granted the honour she was bestowing upon us. The First Communion festivities are a strictly family affair. For tenant farmers to invite their landowners has an old-fashioned ring of courtesy that is by no means common today. Secretly I had hoped for this invitation. But I would never have dared to suggest it. I fancy she saw the happiness that came over me at her words, and I exclaimed:

'Thank you for both of us, Georgette.'

When Georgette talks about her daughter she assumes such an air of ecstasy that I become almost afraid. The things one takes for granted: love, the possession of a child, of a house, of the piece of land around it. Any one of these things, or all of them together, can be blown away at the first breath of wind. If only her child might not be taken away from her as the house in which we were talking appeared on the verge of being taken away from me. Might she keep her child. Might I keep mine.

'I'm so terribly tired,' said Georgette, picking up the milk can, 'but so very happy.'

She smiled and, passing through the garden gate, started to climb up the orchard, past the blue cedar, its outstretched arms shimmering with the tender growth of spring. I had so constantly thought of it as our son's tree, his and his young wife, Lisette's tree, telling myself that when they had children, as they presumably would have, the children and the most noble of trees would grow up together in this quiet spot where their father was born. Yet suddenly the sight of it now chilled me. The blue cedar, like the house itself, was right in the centre of where the by-pass would run. I felt like the little girl in the fairy story who was running happily up the hill when she stumbled, dropping her milk jug which broke, scattering the precious milk at her feet. My hopes had crashed like hers. How unjustly do certain aspects of progress and technology fall on unsuspecting women who still always, and most bitterly, pay. A man can gather up his belongings and go elsewhere, but a woman's heart lies in her home. This house, which the Germans had respected during the occupation, would be destroyed by the French. It was as if Paris, which the German general Von Choltitz gave orders not to burn and plunder at the moment of his own defeat, were one day to be burned and plundered by the French themselves as, alas, had happened more than once before.

Two or three mornings later I was washing the wool of some jumpers I had unpicked. Many hours of my life were spent in knitting and then unpicking woollen garments. Even those that I started with the greatest enthusiasm eventually ceased to please me. Or perhaps the moth got at them. This time I had unpicked a number of such jumpers in order to use the wool to make a rug for my room with the stout canvas that the shippers had put round several wooden cases dispatched from London. With some of the wool I was now gently washing I had made a pullover for my son to wear at his first school. Subsequently I had unpicked his school pullover and knitted it into a scarf for myself. Now I had unpicked the scarf and the wool would go into my rug.

There was a knock at the kitchen door and, turning round, I saw through the glass panes my young farmer, Jacques Déliquaire. His arrival in the place of Georgette always suggests a crisis, something wrong in the orchard, something that would have to be smoothed over, or perhaps an urgent phone call to the veterinary surgeon for a difficult calving.

'I've come about Georgette,' he said. 'She was taken ill in the night and the doctor, who has already come to see her, wants us to telephone to the surgeon at the nursing home in Deauville for an appointment. He thinks it's acute appendicitis. Fancy it having to happen now! With less than three weeks to Brigitte's First Communion!'

I went to the telephone and made an appointment for three o'clock, having failed to persuade the surgeon to see her before lunch. Jacques said that he would drive her there and that the doctor had not suggested there was any great urgency. Indeed, except for any repercussions it might have on the coming ceremony, he appeared to be taking her sudden attack rather lightly, and though I was unwilling to alarm him I tried to point out that acute appendicitis must be treated with the utmost seriousness.

Towards eight o'clock Jacques came back to say that it had indeed proved more urgent than he had anticipated. 'As a matter of fact', he said, 'this was not her first attack, but I didn't attach much importance to the others. If one had to call a doctor every time a woman complains about not feeling well there would be no end to it!' He laughed, thankful, I expect, to feel the worst was over. 'I'm never ill,' he said, 'that's why I don't always understand.'

The weather had turned warmer and, though I seldom visited our more distant meadows and woods, I felt a sudden urge to see one of our hayfields which we called the Burgundy. The comparative rarity of these tours of inspection worried me. But the house, the flower and the kitchen garden already exhausted me. In the days of easy labour I would doubtless have had a maid, a gardener and a handyman to cut the wood and feed the furnace. I had none of these, so that when I did feel justified in taking an hour off I preferred to run down to the beach rather than to walk through the lanes or across our hilly orchards, as my mother loved to do. One could scarcely walk fifty yards without it being up a hill or down one. She used to discover the loveliest things and rejoice in them. But more often than not now I come upon some form of destruction that puts me in a state of tension, and that I do my best to avoid. There is no point in tilting against windmills. Moreover as often as not the windmill makes itself invisible. For instance, the hay was becoming tall and lovely in the Burgundy as well as in the much larger Molière, which all along its southern slope is bordered by overhanging branches of beech, ash and wild cherry. These form part of a small triangular wood whose fringes I forbid in contract to be cut. The hay was tall and beautiful and the grass was once full of tall daisies and other fragrant, colourful wild flowers that gave it a particular sweetness when cut, but these had now quite disappeared. I could not have gathered enough ox-eye daisies to fill a vase in the living-room. If beauty is a useless thing I had no right to formulate even secretly a regret, nor to feel sad to notice the increasing disappearance of the wild rose and honeysuckle from my hedges. Like even the most modest of landowners, they were becoming redundant. I would have to bring my scissors back unused. With Georgette away at hospital I would peep in at the farm.

The house was a long low building with spacious lofts under a red-tiled roof which continued uninterruptedly over barns, a buttery, a garage, stables and cowsheds. At right angles were the cider presses, vats, farm sheds and so on. In the courtyard were piggeries, small sheds for calves, rabbit hutches and cages for the tame pheasants which so many local farmers insisted on rearing. Beyond a kitchen garden was a beautiful little building which had once been a wash-house, but I don't think that Georgette had ever boiled her linen in the great cauldron or used the place for its original purpose. Now that she had her electric washing-machine, I feared the wash-house would be put to uses that might well hasten its downfall in the world. A pity, for it was a story-book house.

The hens, ducks and geese scattered at my approach, and the dogs barked. How different everything looked. A great part of the courtyard facing the buttery was hidden under a giant tent, like a circus tent, at the opening of which two persons were talking. One of them was a man employed by the town hall to mend lanes and ditches and to trim overhanging hedges, a function which gave him the title of *cantonnier*. The other was Mme Bessel, Georgette's rather formidable looking but gentle-voiced milk-maid who, with her crippled husband, lived in a cottage which our son now owned and which formed part of some land he had bought from the former Mme Anger estate.

I was greeted with great politeness and shown over the tent with its long table to seat some fifty people. The food would be cooked or heated in the buttery and served to the guests piping hot. M. Levannier and Jacques, with the help of the *cantonnier*, had put up the tent and built sturdy wooden frames to hold the awnings. Thus they had been able to cut down considerably the expenses of this vast undertaking that would continue almost uninterruptedly for three days and three nights.

Mme Bessel exclaimed that it was time to go milking, and she began fastening the great milk churns on either side of the donkey's leather saddle. The milking saddle was as fine a piece of work, all made by hand, as you would find anywhere in France or even in Spain. It was a fine sight to see Mme Bessel setting off for some distant orchard with her donkey walking sedately beside her and the milk churns securely fastened to each side of the saddle.

A day or two later about tea time I drove to the Deauville Clinic. There are several modern buildings standing behind tall wrought-iron gates on their own land to the right of the main highway as you enter the city. One of these I knew to be the clinic. I was nearly brought here in a thunderstorm when things went wrong while I was having my baby in the farmhouse before the war. As I should certainly have died on the way I never felt a particular urge to visit it, but on this occasion I was bound by a social obligation which I could not escape. Besides, I was longing to see Georgette in her best nightdress in a white cot and to ask her all about her great experience. I stopped the car in front of the first of those large modern buildings. This, I decided, must be the clinic.

I rang a bell and was welcomed by a beautiful aged nun who exclaimed with the sweetest and most understanding smile: 'No, no, we are not the nursing sisters. The St Joseph Clinic is the large building next to ours. We are the hospice.'

'Forgive me, sister,' I said. ' I am really sorry to have brought you to the door and all the more so because I'm afraid that you're going to be disturbed a second time. I sent my husband to buy some chocolates for the patient we are about to visit, and I'm pretty certain he is going to make the same mistake as I did.'

'Well,' said the aged nun, 'we shall be delighted to see him. We are always glad to welcome a visitor and put him on the right road.'

She led me down the gravel path to the big wrought-iron gates, and I marvelled at the beauty of her brown robes, like those of the monks one used to see travelling on foot from village to

village, and I looked at her rosary dangling from her waist and
her lovely gentle smile.

The doorkeeper at the clinic was a good deal less amiable.
Apparently I had arrived at the wrong entrance, but refusing to
be intimidated I demanded the number of Georgette's room and
ran up some stairs to find it.

Georgette was just as I expected to find her, looking splendid
in her nylon nightdress, more rested than I had seen her for a
long time. Seated on hard chairs by the bed were Mme Levannier
with her little son Bruno on her knees, and Mme Levannier's
sister who had been on holiday at the farm since the beginning of
the week. We were very gay, especially when my husband arrived
with the chocolates, having first gone, as I suspected, to the
hospice where he was received with much kindness and laughter
by the sisters. When poor Georgette laughed she exclaimed:
'Please don't make me laugh again. It hurts!' So we all tried to
broach more serious subjects.

'Preparations are going along apace at your farm!' I said to
Georgette. 'The tent looks splendid.'

'Just think how fortunate I am to have had this operation now,'
she exclaimed. 'I'll just do it. You'll see! Indeed I think the rest
will do me good. Did Jacques tell you that we went to Paris last
week to buy his new suit and my outfit for the church? All I
need to do now is to have my hair styled for the great day!'

She looked and doubtless felt like a real princess. What she had
dreamed of would come true after all.

Sunday dawned fine but very cold.

I caught myself dressing for the religious service with as much
care as Brigitte's mother was doubtless dressing at the farm.
When I was younger I dressed out of pride. Now it was more
frequently out of respect. I put on a two-piece that Mlle Chanel
had made for me, and over this a dark mink jacket I had bought
in London, a mink so dark as to be almost jet. I could not have
done more to honour a queen. Youth in a woman is better, but it
carries with it hesitation, imitation and timidity. And what is the
good of weeping over the smashed jug of milk.

The church smelt of incense, and the sun sent shafts of light
through the stained-glass windows. Massively built, the church

dated from the late nineteenth century and closely resembled any English church of the same period. Church and village must have grown up together. Someone who collected picture postcards gave me one of the village taken in about 1900, which showed the congregation coming out from Mass on a Sunday morning at the height of the summer season. The narrow street and even the shops had hardly changed: only the formal clothes of the men, their gold watch chains and long moustaches, the tight belted waists and long skirts of the women, the little girls with their straight bodices and starched skirts, the boys in sailor hats.

Today the service had already started, and as I walked slowly up the side aisle I could see all the girl communicants dressed like brides and the boys bedecked in white robes, unnaturally shy and quiet. The parents were massed in the front pews. Jacques Déliquaire, his skin burnt by wind and sun to the redness of Elizabethan brick, was wearing his brand-new blue suit bought a fortnight earlier during that expedition to Paris; Georgette was in a salmon dress and matching coat and wearing an immense white hat that gave her a 'between the wars' appearance. Until then I doubt if I had ever seen her otherwise than bare-headed or wearing a printed scarf over her head as she helped Jacques to call the cows together, fork up the newly mown hay or gather the apples in November from the long damp grass. The hair stylist had dyed her hair a reddish hue and cut it so short behind that one saw a white line above the sunburnt skin. There is singing, and Mme Leclerc, a very pretty widow who holds an important post at the Mairie, sings solo in her lovely soprano voice these lines that the communicants echo in unison with the priest:

> 'Here is the Lamb so gentle
> Bread of angels
> From heaven He descends on us
> Let us adore Him.'

These lines that appear singularly lacking in literary merit as I put them down on paper, almost religious doggerel, have yet followed me with haunting repetition since my own girlhood. I must have heard them first on my mother's knee in Montmartre, at the very first school I attended, at the declaration of war in 1914 when, with tricolours flying and women weeping, the poilus went off so joyously to the bloodiest carnage in history. I heard them again when our school was requisitioned, when the first badly wounded soldier came back, died and was put in a coffin over which pious hands spread the French flag.

As these thoughts passed through my mind Jacques and Georgette looked proudly at their daughter who had joined in the singing. When Jacques was little and his father was my farmer I used to see him gaily crossing my home orchard and, if he wasn't whistling, he would be singing at the top of his boyish voice. Now that he is grown up, he criss-crosses the orchard on his tractor, cutting down the weeds that the cows have refused to eat, but he doesn't sing any more. Nor does Brigitte ever sing. Instead she and her friends gravely listen to pop music on a record-player.

At the end of the service the communicants walk in procession round the church and then the great doors are flung open and, to the sound of the peeling of bells, they and their parents stream out into the sunshine where the photographers are waiting for them. M. Larue the butcher stands in his white apron at the door of his shop with Mme Larue and their pretty daughter Martine. Motor-cars start up and disappear past the memorial of two world wars. Both wars sometimes give one the impression of being temporarily under a cloud.

Only a few ageing men who wear forgotten medals and gather in pathetic knots each Bastille Day remember the first one anyway. Youth sniggers and turns aside. What young man wants to be reminded of the glory of Verdun when Marshal Pétain, its hero, came to such a miserable end because of the great soldier's political role in the Second World War? Dead, was he not still banished? As indeed were so many builders of a North African empire, now reduced to the rank of traitors though soon to be pardoned. There had been so much to admire. There was so little left. The British who had poured out their life blood during the battle of the Somme had become a race to be pitied. The Canadians, other than certain separatists, were not much better, and a few of them who a short time back had come to bask in the great deeds of their fathers during the battle of Vimy found themselves forgotten and alone. Even the allied invasion of Normandy had become an awkward, difficult chapter of recent history that it might be better to minimize in future textbooks. The Americans, as could be read on many a city wall, on many a seaside breakwater, were murderers. Only Mao was great. Only the North Vietnamese were heroes.

The little girls in their bridal clothes, with lace veil and book in hand, the little boys in those rather absurd white gowns that made them appear the very antithesis of their natural aggressiveness, were being collected by parents and taken off to wherever their particular festivities would begin. They had not yet reached the age of rigid scholastic examination and weeding out, of the struggle to find a place in a society uneasily moving from Gaullism to Communism, from too much liberty to too little.

But as I walk briskly through it today, our village is on holiday, and this immense happiness, this throwing aside of cares, this general optimism combine to lighten my step. Outside the church I had kissed Brigitte, radiant in her bridal veil. Georgette and Jacques had said to me:

'We are counting on both of you this evening, Ma'am Henrey.'

The weather turned colder towards evening, so much so that it looked as if it would be a night of wind, rain and ice. As darkness fell I stood watching the strange contrast of the tall fir trees that formed a mighty curtain at the bottom of the kitchen garden, with the delicate blossom of pear and cherry in the orchards. For a little while we sat by the log fire in the big room watching television, and it was almost with regret that we left its comfortable warmth. The room was full of flowers, the first lilac of the year, tall blue irises and a silver bowl of lilies-of-the-valley which seemed to thrive under the rose trees in front of the house.

'What a night to go and be festive in a marquee tent,' I exclaimed as we drove out of the orchard into the damp loneliness of the lane, our headlights picking out the animals grazing by the holly hedge. We turned into the the farmyard and found ourselves suddenly plunged into all the effervescence of this great occasion; our young robust farmer, looking very important in his new suit, directing the traffic, Georgette in her salmon-coloured dress holding court by the white barrier where so often I had seen her throwing grain to her chickens; lanterns flickering, torches throwing beams of light, servants running about with dishes, children playing hide-and-seek in the dark amongst the guests, friend calling to friend, relation discovering relation, why—I knew that this was going to be a night that I would never forget.

I think they had been waiting for us, because I had timed our arrival with great precision, and so now the flap of the long tent was drawn aside and we found ourselves projected into the gaiety of this huge family gathering, shaking hands, recognizing, being recognized, blinking a little under the strong lights, but to my relief beautifully warmed by electric fires placed at intervals all along both sides of the tent. Silver and glassware gleamed on freshly ironed linen tablecloths, and all the sides of the tent were garlanded with spring flowers and wreaths of evergreen so that one had the impression of being in a hothouse in Kew Gardens.

The grandmothers and the aunts are all at the top end of the table, the end nearest the buttery, a trifle self-conscious in their best Sunday clothes, but so happy and proud that their sweet, gentle faces are a joy to look upon. I go over to talk to them all in turn, to hear all their latest news, to be questioned about my son, so busy and important in New York, whom they will always think of as a little boy in a bright red pullover who flew away from our orchards at the age of eight to make a film. They were all so happy to bask in his short moment of fame. Nothing will convince them that he is really grown up. Brigitte, the star of this present round of festivities, her cheeks pink with excitement, still wearing her wedding dress, her gold watch shining on her little wrist, gold chains and pious medals hanging from her slender neck, hurries from group to group, blushing with the pleasure of feeling herself admired. The presents are set out on a table in a corner of the tent behind the grandmothers and the aunts. Grandmother Madeleine Déliquaire's electric record-player is greatly commented upon. The largest of the gifts, it stands beside the smallest which is mine, a white purse in crochet work which I made for her and which I filled to the brim with those beautiful real silver coins that the French mint put into limited circulation at the height of its government's proud, almost arrogant, gold-backed-currency haughtiness. So many of us had forgotten what real silver coins look and feel like that there was a curious, sensual pleasure in handling these. Even the United States had ceased minting real silver coins.

Our chairs were at the end of the table farthest away from the grandmothers, aunts, uncles, Jacques and Georgette and their daughter. This gave us an opportunity of meeting distant relations or intimate friends of the family whom we had not met before. I gave myself over to this task with enthusiasm. The prettiness of the table with the white hydrangeas, the tapestry effect of the evergreens and spring flowers on the sides of the tent and the general air of warmth, cosiness and anxiety to please had put me in a receptive frame of mind.

My neighbour, a Frenchman, introduced himself as the second husband of Malenka (the Russian equivalent of my own name), a first cousin of Rosalie who was born as she was in the wheat plains of the Ukraine. Malenka leaned forward and smiled. Her husband had worked in the armament factory of Le Creusot, a simple workman (he was anxious to stress the humble nature of his position) principally engaged in making guns. He was now retired and exclaimed in a burst of honest enthusiasm: 'It's wonderful to be retired on a pension. Don't let any man tell you the contrary! Heavens, I've worked hard enough. I deserve it.'

His, of course, had been a reserved occupation at the beginning of the last war, but when the French army collapsed German agents went to the foundry to ask for volunteers to work in Germany. 'As I felt in no way responsible for what had happened to my country,' my neighbour said, 'and knowing that if I didn't work I would starve, I was glad to volunteer.' He was sent successively to the Ruhr, to Hanover and to Hamburg. 'This experience opened my eyes to a good many unsuspected truths,' he said; 'the greater dignity of the German steelworker, the cordial relations he enjoyed with his superiors, the feeling that he was somebody who really mattered. Our wages were high and life in Germany at that time was relatively cheap. I had no trouble in coming to terms with my new existence. Some foreign workers found it difficult to get used to German food. I, on the contrary, enjoyed it all the more because it was so different. When one owns nothing in the country of one's birth, one is less likely when abroad to harbour prejudices. I was certainly feeding better than my compatriots in the occupied zone. The Germans were friendly and clean, and the room in which I lodged shone like a new pin. The only thing I found difficult to get accustomed to were German beds with those balloon shaped bedclothes that can't be tucked in.'

The feast was starting, and the first of the wines was being poured into one of the many glasses ranged in front of every guest. There was to be a different wine for every course, and it suddenly struck me how lamentably ignorant I was about such gastronomical details. My neighbour, as a sign of abstinence, turned his glass down. I think he was still asking himself why exactly he had so enjoyed himself working for the Nazis while France was occupied. He said:

'Maybe I should have told you that I was then a widower without children. Such a violent change of scene, such a different way of living, such a lot of money to spend, combined to give me a second youth. Though I was over forty I felt as if I were twenty again, just starting out in life!'

Should I have been shocked? This, I reflected, was precisely what made it so difficult for a person like myself who lived in London under the fierce patriotism of Winston Churchill, and a whole nation welded together in common endeavour, to understand what was happening across the Channel. The intricate cross-currents in every man's soul. We thought too much in terms of collaborators versus Resistance. Now, so long afterwards, the nicest people in this village were constantly asking themselves if continued occupation by the Germans might not have saved them from the reefs ahead. This might even be at the root of their lack of gratitude to the British and the Americans for saving them!

But on whose side are any of their politicians today? While the Communist deputies remained quiescent, who was it who invited first Khrushchev, then Kosygin to march triumphantly through French factories while the workers waved the Red Flag and sang the 'Internationale'? Who toured the Communist countries by jet, proclaiming such exuberant goodwill? How is it that a government, which so many Frenchmen look upon as reactionary, can so often on French television show propaganda films for China's cultural revolution, or give interviews with Communist guerillas in South America, or sing the praises of the troops of Ho Chi Minh when they invade South Vietnam, or denounce night after night the Americans as perpetrating a crime against humanity?

'Malenka, my wife, was a widow when I married her,' my neighbour was now saying, rousing me from my short reverie. 'Her son is that fine young man over there with the child in his

arms. He is a brilliant civil engineer who is engaged just now
in building a dam over the River Rance at St Malo. He and his
wife have two children. The youngest whom you see in his arms
was unwell before we left and we really ought not to have come,
but Georgette and Rosalie would have been so very disappointed.'

'Did you come from far?' I asked.

'From St Malo,' he answered. 'It's a tidy way.'

'I know the road,' I said.

This was the road we took in 1940 when we fled, my husband,
my baby and I, before the advancing Germans. The last ship
to leave France brought us safely, but minus my mother, to
Southampton.

I asked Malenka if to her knowledge she still had any of her
family in the Ukraine. She said yes, she had a brother living at
Kiev. She said she would have liked to go and visit him, but the
risk of not being able to come back to France was too great.
'He and I are both sixty now,' she added. 'We are too old to make
plans for the future.'

How had all these Ukrainians come to Western Europe in the
first place? Rosalie had worked for a time in Berlin, where she
picked up German. She later arrived (she was never quite sure
how) in our village where she was hired by Mme Anger, a master-
ful widow, who owned some thirty acres of land adjoining my
own. It was here that she had met Georgette's father who was
killed in the war shortly after their marriage. Malenka said that
when she was still living in the vicinity of Kiev, a Ukrainian girl
she knew who had already emigrated to the West spent a holiday
in France, and wrote home saying that in a certain village near
Deauville she had come upon a compatriot called Rosalie.
'And', cried Malenka, 'imagine my excitement when I learnt that
this Rosalie was none other than my cousin Rosa!' They immediately started a correspondence, and that is how Malenka arrived in
Normandy.

'Learning to speak French was not easy,' she went on, 'so it
was a joy to have Cousin Rosa here so that we could talk and joke
together in Ukrainian. Now that I am married to a Frenchman'—
Malenka glanced lovingly at her husband—'I have no option,
but it still gives me pleasure to come here and have a real, good
gossip in Ukrainian with Cousin Rosa.'

'She says she has no option,' broke in her husband, 'but as you will have noticed she speaks very good French. Of course she will have fewer opportunities to speak her native tongue as our children and grandchildren take roots here. She will be the first to admit that there are compensations. You should see our pretty little house at Rheims, that we were given in exchange for the apartment in which we lived while we were still working. Our garden is large enough to provide us with vegetables and flowers, but not too large for us to manage easily. Malenka finds it impossible to remain idle for more than a few moments at a time. She does washing and ironing for some of the younger house-wives whose husbands work in nearby offices. With the money she earns she buys toys for her grandchildren. As for me, I work in the garden, I play bowls with other men of my age, and all I would ask is for it to go on for as long as possible. That's why I do what I can to keep fit. We have been offered no fewer than five different wines so far this evening. You may have noticed that I have refused them all. Later on I don't say that I won't accept a drop of champagne, but only in moderation. The menu is always very abundant on these occasions. At least ten courses. I gather that the next course will consist of guinea fowl.' He had put on his spectacles and was examining the white and silver card. 'Well, I shall pass that over. As indeed I shall the sweet. A man should exercise the same discipline on himself as if he were a soldier.'

His wife Malenka laughed affectionately. She had the same mischievous laugh as Rosalie, a wrinkling of the Slav features into merriment. She made me think of the women I had seen in Moscow and Leningrad, rotund like the coloured wooden figurines sold to children.

The woman facing us on the other side of the table had been following our conversation for some moments, and now she proceeded to tell us about her own worries. She said to my neighbour:

'Your discipline for remaining fit entails no great hardship. My problem for remaining alive is how never to put undue strain on my heart. I have to pay for the slightest excess, sometimes by days and nights of suffering.'

She was a relatively young and unusually pretty woman with two boys by a first marriage and a ten-year-old girl, called Catherine, by her present husband. Her second marriage, she tells us, is as radiantly happy as her first one was miserable.

The husband, whose agreeable features were partly hidden by a white hydrangea decorating the table, was a native of our Pays d'Auge, son of a long line of highly competent and successful owner-farmers, the Orleachs, some of whom had moved to Paris, others remaining on their rich orchards, leading simple, useful lives. This particular Orleach had done his military service in Indo-China with Jacques. They were 'buddies', and whenever Jacques and Georgette went to Paris they stayed with them.

'I know what it feels like', said pretty Mme Orleach, 'to remain balanced precariously between life and death. It was expected that I should die. Only my youth saved me. As if the tribulations I endured were not sufficient, my husband chose this moment to abandon me with our two boys.

'My present husband, who appears to be sharing an excellent joke with Jacques, came to my help and pulled me out of the well of despair. As soon as I got my divorce he married me.

'Thanks to this wonderful man, it is as if I had died and been born again. Life is opening out like the petals of a flower. My sons are happy with him—as for my little Catherine, the daughter of such wonderful, unbelievable happiness. . . .'

This was where the story took an unexpected turn.

I had already seen Catherine with Brigitte and had been struck by her slender, appealing beauty. She looked like a nymph dancing on air. Imagine a creature whose every movement was elegant, with dark lustrous hair tied at the back into a pony-tail. The two little girls had brought the milk to me one morning in the place of Georgette. Brigitte had explained that it was her best friend. Sometimes Brigitte went to spend a week with Catherine in Paris; sometimes Catherine would come to spend a week with Brigitte on the farm.

What nobody had told me was that Catherine at the age of ten had turned into such a remarkable figure-skater that she was being groomed for world stardom. She was being taught, as my own son had been taught at the same age, in fact two years younger, the stringent discipline of forming part of a complex machine. The fact that one was the central figure in a film and the other in a great expanse of ice made little difference. A lesson in humility, in punctuality, in politeness to others, an early appreciation for the talents of those by whom they are surrounded, this is what hard work and the capacity for taking pains give so generously to a child, any child who has the good fortune to be shown at so early an age how men and woman toil for a livelihood. There is a good chance that later they will never know boredom. 'I have only brought Catherine for a little while,' said her mother. 'I'm afraid all these good things, even if she desired them, would have to be turned away. Little girl skaters must not depart from a savagely controlled diet, and tomorrow morning she must be back in Paris. The rink is being iced over specially for her. She must keep nobody waiting.'

'Do many people ask you how it all began?' I queried. 'I myself was once so often obliged to answer a similar question.'

'The story lacks romance,' said her mother. 'When she was barely six we all went to watch some figure-skating at a Paris rink. On our return home, as I was helping Catherine to undress, she said: "Mother, I have discovered my vocation. I want to skate."

'I thought it was merely a child's whim as if, after going to the circus, she had dreamed of becoming a glamorous besequined tight-rope dancer, or as if she had wanted to become a ballerina after going to the pantomime. However, I must admit that the first time we put skates on her, she flew off as if she had never worn anything else. So perhaps there was something more in her than a little girl's natural desire to emulate what she had seen. Wanting by itself might not have been enough. What do you think? Is it at all possible that she was born with an ability to disport herself elegantly on ice, as another girl might be born with that mysterious something needed to produce a good actress or a successful opera singer?

'Many people scoff at child prodigies. And yet there's hardly a family in France that is not convinced that its own little Jack or Jill is so clever that he or she must be given a university education, even though the budding genius hasn't the vaguest idea what it wants to do in life! Well, it's something to have a mind of your own at the age of six. Catherine's chosen profession is tough. I have seen her little body covered with black bruises where she has fallen down on the ice, but I never once heard her complain. Occasionally she takes such a punishment that when I undress her at night I wonder if I have the right to let her go on with it. But in the morning, when she runs on to the ice, her features are transfixed with joy. Don't imagine that her lessons are neglected.

She studies twice as hard as other girls, so that nobody can ever accuse her of neglecting her schoolwork in favour of her profession. We spend our winters at Chamonix. There's an excellent school there and we have bought an apartment so that she can enjoy the family life that she would have in Paris. If anybody complicates her own life it is I, her mother, because we have a business in Paris and I am obliged to cut myself in two. But I am so happy to be alive, so proud of Catherine, so in love with my husband, that I would cut myself into six if that were necessary.

'How a woman's existence can suddenly alter!

'Ten or more years ago I had a small shop in a seaside village. Everything was more than peaceful. Today, because of Catherine, my life has become a veritable whirlwind—journeys to distant places, carefully drawn-up time-tables, championships, hopes, deceptions and this constant, ferocious diet, the daily nightmare of the scales. Gone from the family menu are those delicious sauces we were once so partial to. Lean steaks grilled, or even raw when she needs to make some special effort. We have given her this little holiday and she is having a wonderful time with Brigitte, but I don't need to tell her to be careful about what she eats. There is nothing about her of the naughty girl just waiting for mother's back to be turned. She's even stricter about her diet than I am. And this brings me to what is perhaps the most telling reflection of all. It would be, to my mind, quite impossible for parents to impose an artistic career on any child who was not born with the will and the ability to succeed.'

'Well,' I said, 'this year you have brought your Catherine to Brigitte's First Communion. When will Brigitte be attending Catherine's?'

'Ah!' she exclaimed, the joy suddenly leaving her. 'There's the rub. This is my great unhappiness. The one question I cannot solve.'

'How so?'

'In Paris our parish priest is explicit. Either Catherine must abandon her career or she will have to forego her First Communion. There are no two ways about it.'

'Other little girls——'

'Perhaps, but in his opinion professional figure skating is a form of exhibitionism. My clever, hard-working, gifted daughter, therefore, must be robbed of the Holy Sacrament, even though it would not be denied to an actress or a film star.'

Trying to understand the priest's objections I asked thoughtfully:

'What is the position of little girls who attend the state ballet school? The future dancers of the Paris Opera House?'

'I have inquired,' said Catherine's mother. 'They do not fall under this cruel interdiction.'

'Yet there would appear to be a great similarity?'

All our end of the table had suddenly become aware of the dilemma. A great hush had fallen over at least a dozen guests who were obviously consulting their own consciences before giving an opinion.

'Could you not have Catherine prepared at Chamonix in the winter,' I asked 'so that she could take her First Communion there? Would one priest necessarily be of the same opinion as another? You say you own an apartment at Chamonix. You are therefore officially a resident. That would appear to me an honest way of trying to solve the problem?'

'I have tried,' said Catherine's mother. 'The priest at Chamonix has referred me to my parish priest in Paris. One would not do it without the consent of the other. I fear there is no way out. I am heartbroken.'

Now Malenka spoke up.

'You must address yourself directly to His Holiness the Pope!' she exclaimed. 'At the time of his projected wedding to a French girl, my son was faced with a problem which appeared just as insoluble. Our parish priest was adamant—within his rights, as he saw them, but adamant. Not that I blamed him. But for me, for my son, for my future daughter-in-law, and for the children they might have—whom indeed they now have—the matter was too grave for me not to appeal to the highest court. So what did I do? I wrote to His Holiness the Pope.'

The guests within listening distance were now turned towards this little Ukrainian woman with her flat nose and round features. She had become the centre of attention. We were anxious to hear the circumstances. She said:

'My son was baptized into the Russian Orthodox Church. This was the faith of my people and I could not then foresee what complications would arise when he grew up in a foreign land and became part of it, forgetting even the language of his forbears. But that is exactly what does happen to our children. They forget even our language. I have already told you that my cousin Rosa remains one of the few people with whom I can converse happily in Ukrainian.

'Well, my son at the time of his marriage to a French girl was not able to produce a certificate of First Communion, and the parish priest declared that in the circumstances he would not be able to celebrate their wedding. My future daughter-in-law, however, was very understandably unwilling to enter into a marriage that had not taken place in church. We did not know what to do. If my son had persuaded his fiancée to forgo the religious ceremony, then they themselves as well as the children born of the marriage would live under a cloud. So, as we were simple people and had the good fortune to live in a free country, a country in which its citizens had the right to do as they thought fit without fear of being punished or imprisoned, we wrote to His Holiness Pope John XXIII. We set out the facts of the case asking for permission very clearly, and promised that the children would be brought up as good Catholics. Our case was considered and the permission we sought was granted. We even went to Rome to receive the Pope's benediction. When he died, this great and just man whom all the world admired, we grieved him as a friend. So you see, it is wrong to let oneself sink into despair. If a thing is important one must persist. Ask, and if you meet with a rebuff, go on tirelessly asking. I feel sure that if you were to do as we did you will succeed.'

As the meal advanced the children grew tired of sitting still and got down from their places to join in a helter-skelter round the long table. Brigitte, in her virginal white wedding dress, and Catherine were followed by more than a score of small nephews and nieces.

Their rowdiness heralded the moment when the festivities to celebrate a solemn religious ceremony began to descend from the sacred to the bawdy. This has happened right through the ages, especially in remote country districts. Bawdy songs, barrack-room jesting and practical jokes inevitably take over. The children take a delight in handing sugar to the grown-ups who discover when they drop it in their coffee that it turns into a frog or a toad, or perhaps a goldfish or a sea anemone. The children try to frighten or scare us, and their peals of laughter create a sort of pandemonium while at the same time the men try to shock the women by ribaldry of an inoffensive, Elizabethan character. By now, none of us, not even the grandmothers, after at least ten different kinds of wine had been passed round, would be such spoil-sports as to hinder the fun. We are all just a little drunk, including Malenka and her abstemious husband. Some of the men, smoking Italian cigars, go out for a breather into the cold damp darkness of the courtyard. The children place detonators on their chairs so that when they sit down again the rumbling noise thus produced makes the first ones, unaware of the joke, blush with embarrassment. It is curious that even when those of us who have heard our parents tell of such happenings, or read about them in the books of George Sand, find ourselves for the first time in this flash-back to an age of buggy-carts, oil lamps and tallow candles, we hesitate between fascination and horror. How can it be true that such frightening modernity as the bulldozing of a great motor road can be equated with a life that goes back with such fidelity to the past? This child who is pulling at my sleeve, trying to inflict some practical joke on me, is a son of Roger, Jacques's brother, who works in the village. The wedding lunch which took place at a hostelry, now defunct, in our village allowed me to witness something that I had heard my grandmother at Blois talk about but which I had never noticed with my own eyes before. At Roger's wedding lunch there were long trestle tables for the guests with the bride and groom seated half way along. When I was very young there were no tablecloths large enough to cover so great an expanse when such wedding lunches took place on farms. The bride's family brought out the precious linen bedsheets, beautifully ironed and glazed for the occasion. They were so wide they reached down to the ground on either side of the table. Guests had to put their knees where they could. Towards the end of these seemingly interminable meals, when everybody had imbibed liberally, a practical joke was played which must have dated from the Middle Ages. One of the groom's best friends would go down on all fours and, hidden by the sides of the sheet, creep slowly between the legs of the guests until he reached those of the bride. Then, plunging his hands under her wedding gown, he would wrench off a garter, spring up on to the table and display it to the entire cheering party. Now this I actually witnessed at Roger's wedding at that now defunct hostelry in our village, and it amused me to think that here was one of Roger's children pulling at my sleeve.

The traditional cake, the *pièce-montée* or set piece of the party, now made its appearance. Wide at the base and surrounded by small cream puffs, it became progressively narrower as it tapered up to the apex of the cone-shaped edifice, the whole magnificent confection sticky with burnt caramel.

Shortly before one o'clock my husband and I took our leave. As little Catherine was carried off by her parents to bed I wondered what solution would be found to the problem of her religious upbringing. The lane smelt delicious as raindrops from the over-hanging trees splashed on to the roof of the car. The cows in M. Levannier's orchard gazed at us inquisitively. The ox-eye daisies and vetch gleamed under a white moon. We were still in the depths of the country, but I could not help wondering for how long.

# 4

AT THE end of her summer holidays the previous September I had driven my friend Simone Marchand to the Paris train. Now a professor of mathematics in a school at Clichy, she was born a few doors away from the house in Montmartre where my mother made lace blouses when I was a baby, and came to spend every summer in our village. While we were seated on her luggage waiting for her train to arrive, she confessed to starting this new term with an uncomfortable presentiment. She said that in the academic world there had been for some time the same uneasiness as there had been in the country as a whole before the German invasion of 1940, a sense of impending tragedy.

In fact what Simone Marchand experienced was an intensification of the malaise that was increasingly apparent in our village. The strong drive on the part of parents to channel their children, both boys and girls, into scientific and teaching careers, was to a great extent motivated by a desire to improve their social status. It was a movement that was powerfully fanned by all political parties of whatever colour. Even the independent farmer of our rich pastures was being made to feel that there was something ugly in the need to milk his cows and till his land. The fact that he was his own master and relatively better off than the rest of the community did not wipe him clean of the ruddiness of his features and the shame of stout boots smeared with cow dung. Georgette dreamed of the day when Brigitte, an elegant schoolmistress, would have travelled socially beyond the state of being constantly behind the tail of the cow, as the saying went in these parts. With almost monotonous regularity, French television sent its young reporters from both the state-owned channels to ask farmers in every province of this still agricultural country if they, their wives, and even more their children, were not tired of lacking the leisure and modern conveniences that the inhabitants of the towns enjoyed.

It was as if the state were eager to push them out of their farms and into the congested towns and cities at an even faster rate than would have happened anyway. This was indeed the case. New blood was needed to help modernize the industries that were not yet able to compete against those of certain countries in the Common Market, let alone that of the contender Britain. At the same time, farms of fewer than a thousand acres, though hitherto the backbone of the country, were now considered uneconomic.

Our small shopkeepers were going through similar troubles. The charm of village life in France continued to rest on a number of anomalies long since swept away in more industrialized nations. We had, for instance, no fewer than three bakers from whom we could buy our favourite kinds of bread, hot from the oven, from six in the morning till nearly nine at night, Saturdays and Sundays included. It is true that on Mondays one of the three might close, but that was immaterial from our point of view. Housewives like myself who had unexpected guests for dinner could run down and buy one of those sweet-smelling French loaves so oven hot that it would burn one's bare arms. In spite of vague assaults by the government, our butchers continued to be so individualistic that if I went to M. Larue for a sirloin, he might in all probability tell me: 'This animal, madam, is from Mme Chaignon's farm, the one below the château.'

The urge for parents such as these to drive their children into the race for higher education was no less keen than among the farmers on the plateau. Simultaneously, of course, came the normal inflow of children from the bourgeoisie, that much maligned class of doctors, chemists, notaries and so on who formed the upper crust of village life. Thus the farms were losing the farmers and the farmers' wives of tomorrow, the master bakers and the butchers, with very few exceptions (M. Larue was one) were urging their children to abandon the ancient trade of their fathers and join in the academic scramble, while the same thing was happening to the saddler who made such beautiful leather shoes and handbags, and to the blacksmith who had learned from his father how to keep our farm tools in such wonderful condition. As a consequence the village became a place of frustration and jagged nerves every autumn at examination time. Would dear Tommy get through, or would his mother never dare to show her face again in public?

The plain fact was that the structure of French education had not yet adapted itself to the immense revolution that was taking place. The abuse of the examination system was no more popular with teaching staffs than with parents and children. But there it was, and what was, must be. The same thing was brazenly practised in certain Communist countries. British and American students did not need to have anything like this frenzy. The reason was not far to seek. Universities in Britain and America are not asked by their governments to eliminate at the end of the first or second year from between one-third to one-half of all their undergraduates! But this was what happened in France. In not allowing universities to limit the intake of undergraduates by initial selection, the Minister put upon them the obligation of weeding out this staggering percentage of students during their degree courses.

The fury and disappointment of parents who saw their children cast out from these august institutions was not pretty to see. In a society in which there is virtually no place for the young man or the young woman who lacks the necessary academic qualifications, elimination is virtually the end of every hope. It would have been better for the farmer's son to remain with his father behind the tail of the cow, or for the baker to teach his boy the secrets of his trade. But after a year or two years at the university there is no going back to the simple life. Despair is an excellent breeding place for those waves of Maoist propaganda that not only infect our television screens but sweep across classrooms and modern cement quadrangles.

Every Friday I used to call at the bank. As with the shops in our village, its hours of opening were elastic. Often it was open till seven at night. Helen, the pretty dark-haired cashier, was the daughter of our pork butcher. By a strange coincidence her father had done his military service in the same fort above Nice in which my father Émile had done his.

The main street in our village is so narrow at its busiest section that it was virtually impossible for two cars to pass each other. Now, therefore, it has become a one-way street. I like the narrow effect, which is about the only thing that gives character to the centre of the village, making its late nineteenth-century ugliness less pronounced. At the corner of the main street and the rue de la Mer is an enchanting haberdasher's shop. When we first came to the village this shop was a small bazaar where children bought shrimping nets, pails and spades. The owner died and the place was bought by a Mme Alin, who used one half for an old-fashioned haberdashery. Its sleepy interior was reminiscent of something out of *Alice in Wonderland*. Her husband used the other half for the sale and repair of bicycles. When M. Alin died his widow sold the shop and went to live in a pretty house by the police station.

We greatly feared that the shop where we bought our needles and thread would again change the nature of its business. But no, it was not only to remain a haberdashery but become larger, comprising not merely Mme Alin's side but also that in which her husband had sold and mended bicycles. The new owners were a relatively young grandmother, her married daughter, who had a similar establishment in Deauville, and the married daughter's little boy. When his mother or grandmother was in the shop the boy would sit in one of the windows and quietly watch the pageant of the street.

I already knew the grandmother because she had helped Annette Laurent to run her delightful house in the village one summer previously. The shop, relit and modernized, had become an Aladdin's Cave for all the wonders one saw advertised in riotous colour in the women's weekly magazines—the bras, girdles, nylon slips, stockings and every shade of knitting wool, not to mention silk, threads, needles, hairpins and rollers, elastic and lace, eau-de-Colognes and hair sprays and, during the summer months, a colourful display of the latest swimwear.

The shop had been pulled to pieces and rebuilt by her son-in-law, who did such things professionally. But, quite apart from being a model husband, he was one of those rare men who have two entirely distinct but equally important occupations. By day he could turn an old shop into a dazzling new one. By night he worked as a croupier at the casino at Deauville. Said his mother-in-law: 'He takes great care of his hands while doing manual work, for when he has metamorphosed himself at night into an elegant croupier he knows how important it is to show white, well-tended hands.'

She told me how happy her daughter was in this marriage and how the children loved their father who, perhaps because he worked so hard, was always in a good temper. 'In this respect', she said, 'I was less fortunate than she is. My husband left me and my life was suddenly torn apart like a piece of paper, treasured at one moment, tossed aside the next. That is why I went to help Mme Laurent and why now I am so anxious to make this shop a success. Never have there been so many lovely things to tempt women in the shops. And one must not forget that the little girl of today is already the woman of tomorrow. You have no idea how hard it is to please a little girl, even in a village like this one. Gone are the days when a mother would go into a shop and ask for the garment she thought most suitable for her child, in a colour that would not show the dirt. Even the humblest women ruin themselves to buy their children clothes. A woman came in the other day to choose a dress for her little girl of four. I spent nearly half an hour with her while she tried to make up her mind. Suddenly she said to me: "Oh, I do hope my little girl will be satisfied with my choice. If I buy her something and she doesn't like it, she throws it down and stamps on it!"'

One morning I was looking in the shop window and caught sight of a twin-set in shocking pink. As neither the grandmother nor her daughter was in the shop I asked the young assistant to let me see it. She took it out and handed it to me, saying, 'Let me put it in a bag for you so that you can take it home and try it on quietly in front of your own mirror. I know you dislike choosing things in a hurry.'

That is one of the advantages of the little shop.

People at the bank were talking about some student riots at Caen and a meeting of farmers to protest about the falling price of milk. Nobody quite knew what the students were rioting about in that new Caen university that always looked to me so cold and forlorn, but the farmers, it appeared, were worried about their situation in the coming agreements between France and the other members of the Common Market. A café proprietor who had been at Caen the previous day claimed that the students had sung the 'Internationale' and looted some shops.

'It can't have been that serious,' I protested. 'There was nothing on the television news about it.'

'No,' said somebody else. 'There never is.'

The colour of my twin-set is enchanting, but though the label tells me that it is a kind of Shetland I know by the feel that it is not nearly soft enough to have been made by true Scottish hands. Woollies are my special love, and life in London has spoilt me for foreign imitations. I often found myself wondering if people in Britain fully realized the superb quality and relative cheapness of the knitting wools and garments they produce. Even dress materials in our market booths here would never find buyers in England.

As it didn't seem fair to keep the twin-set overnight I took it back to the shop immediately. The young salesgirl, seeing me arrive with the package, could not hide her disappointment. I told her that I found the wool a little rough and she exclaimed:

'Oh, I am sorry. I was quite certain that you would buy it because of the way you raved about the colour. I even took it upon myself to tell a little lie to madame who is in bed with a touch of influenza and earache. She was worried about what would happen here in the shop during her absence. You know how she takes the business to heart, especially as the place is so new. In order to cheer her up I pretended that I had already sold it to you. I said that it proved that she need not worry about leaving me in sole charge of the shop. Well, never mind. I'll put it back in the window, and hope that somebody else will be tempted by the lovely colour.'

'Oh dear,' I cried. 'I feel like buying it just to make the small lie you told your employer come true. I must find another way of making you happy again. If I were to buy the twin-set I would never wear it. So that's not a solution.' I read in the paper about some woman whose dearest wish was to have sufficient five-pound notes to spend every single one of them without a tinge of regret. To be able to dispose of them easily, she said, without the need afterwards to go through a painful process of self-questioning. What troublesome consciences we women have. Her happiness was being sapped, she said, by the monthly instalments on her Paris apartment which her husband was buying over the next twenty or thirty years. They had saddled themselves with a thirty-thousand-pound debt at the time of their wedding. Well, I sympathize with her. I too would like the 'easy' five-pound note so that I could go to the hairdresser any time I fancied, or wander into a fashionable bar in the Champs Elysées and order a glass of champagne and some Russian caviar and hot toast, and be all alone with my own thoughts seated on one of those crimson velour-backed chairs in a warm, comfortable corner with the radio playing softly while the barman stands behind a shiny bar totting up his racing prospects for the *tiercé*. I should like to have the 'easy' five-pound note so that I could walk into Guerlain and buy a large jar of their delicately scented skin food without that moment of hesitation that spoils extravagance; or acquire a deep cut-glass vase for long-stemmed roses, recklessly add several bottles of famous perfumes to an entire range of up-to-date eye make-up, exchange the shoes one is wearing for those elegant green things that look so pretty in the window but which do not really match anything one owns, enter the first church one sees and after a quick prayer push a folded note into the offertory box, and send another anonymously to the woman round the corner who is trying so hard to manage alone with her young daughter.

These desires are a mixture of sentiment and feminine futility, but I'm pretty certain they will find an echo in many other women. Meanwhile I simply can't let this young salesgirl down. I have her on my conscience, but, whereas I am determined to make her smile again, I must do it from my point of view in a strictly reasonable, utilitarian way. I say to her:

'Oh dear, I nearly forgot. I need a new girdle. If you could only tempt me with something useful and yet pretty, I might help you make the sale you boasted about to your employer. From her sickbed she would remain confident in your ability to sell. In fact we would all be satisfied—you, she and I.'

'Fancy you saying that!' she cried, her face wreathed in smiles. 'What a coincidence! We have just received the most enchanting new girdles.'

French television, on both its state-owned networks, could never quite hide its jubilation at the sight of America, modern giant of a nation it both admired and was envious of, getting bogged down in Vietnam, bitterly remembered by Frenchmen as their former Indo-China. Naïvely it may have been too anxious to cast its praises in other directions.

A just sense of pride in French nuclear research, a deep satisfaction that the nation now had its own powerful deterrent, life among the young pilots of those elegant and far-famed Mirage F.1. fighter planes—all these proved excellent and impelling themes for a weekday or Sunday evening television serials. There really was a sense of new-found patriotism. The country wanted to lead, and not just tag along after some powerful Big Brother. In many spectacular ways France had done better than its rich and powerful neighbours. It was on the up and up. In Shanghai traders preferred the French franc to the dollar and the pound. Nobody wants to live for ever in the shadow of defeat and humiliation. If De Gaulle had faults, lack of patriotism was not one of them. A nation likes its leader to speak out loud and clear. De Gaulle's triumphant visit to Russia had achieved what other nations would have liked to do. But what a splendid way the General had with him! His speeches, delivered without a single note, were masterpieces of French prose. His manner was dignified, polite, full of the authority needed in the head of a great state. Olympian? Yes, a little, but not so aloof that crowds in every country did not cheer when he strode beaming among his admirers, shaking hands, his gigantic stature towering above everybody. If Britain had the supreme dignity of a beautiful and still youthful Queen, France felt herself blessed by no ordinary mortal at the helm.

As a fairly normal corollary to this new phase in Franco-Soviet friendship, a spate of Russian films glorifying the early stages of the Russian revolution were brought over. The Red Flag streamed across every television set in the country while French sub-titles translated the violent shouting of great crowds in 1917 seeking to bring down the bourgeois regime. What nights of violence were being fed to us. We prayed they might not prove contagious.

The new and brutal reversal of old alliances was for the most part accepted silently in our village. The almost personal delight that most people took in the Israeli escape from Arab domination was historic and instinctive. The world loves a brave winner. But there was pride also in the knowledge that the most modern of the fighter planes were of French design and make. The change of official heart, doubtless motivated by the government's desire to win oil concessions from the Arab states at the expense of British and American international oil companies, felt like a negation of fair play.

When Georgette and Jacques were not too tired after a long day in the open air, they would watch television in their bedroom. They seldom managed to remain awake to the end of a film, but we all liked those old British and American favourites which brought us romance and pretty dresses.

I liked them exceedingly, though most of them were dubbed, and it was strange to hear Clarke Gable or Audrey Hepburn talking French. During these critical evenings, however, we were subjected to a new approach. Nearly all such films were followed by discussion groups so that the experts could help us interpret the meaning of the film.

This system had the advantage of bringing to the screen men and women who might not otherwise have become known to us. Rectors of universities and professors, for example. In the course of a discussion about a very old film depicting the great Berlin Air Lift, we were introduced to a professor from one of the newer French universities where trouble was already breaking out among the students who lived and studied there.

This erudite, very good-looking man, from whom one might have expected a clear and scholarly exposé of the events which finally obliged the three Western powers to resort to the air lift, broke out on the contrary into an aggressive defence of the Russians for banning rail, road and canal movements from the West into Berlin, quoting from Soviet speeches and documents to uphold his arguments. Was it possible that an exploit in which his own country had joined could be so savagely attacked by a professor in a state university? It was as if he were not French but Russian.

How great was the influence of men like these, men of un-doubted cleverness and charm, on the impressionable youth of the country—these young men and girls seeking an ideal during their university careers. French youth, even more than British youth, were an easy prey, lacking former opportunities of emigrating overseas, experiencing a feeling of claustrophobia in a shrinking world, further hemmed in by their general inability to speak any tongue other than their own. Would such rewriting of history not lead to an erosion of patriotism, or was it merely just one more excuse to discredit America?

The Gaullist regime was building new universities apace, but somehow, in spite of those television serials, in spite of the Mirage F.1. fighter planes, the Bomb and the advent of the Common Market, incentive was missing. Gone was French Indo-China. Gone were the romantic opportunities and the rich vineyards of Algeria. The riots at Nanterre began to spill over— into the television 8 p.m. news and the puzzled pages of the morning papers.

Still, absurdly, I worried about my house.

If it were really taken away from me, and if I had any money left, and if I were still young enough, I might perhaps build another. In what part of the world? I had no idea. In England? In America? Old Tudor or Elizabethan cottages were picturesque and many people wanted the experience of living in the past, but new houses had built-in cupboards! La Pointe, where I had once wanted to build a house, would have done me very well. My son and daughter-in-law could have lived in my present house. La Pointe is a narrow plateau dominating virtually unspoilt country with glimpses of the sea. In summer cool winds blow over it; in winter it is poetically boisterous. The house I would have built would have consisted of a large kitchen with one huge plate glass window overlooking the south—a place not only in which to cook but also to eat. The living-room would have had immense built-in cupboards of every dimension, for dresses, for coats, for shoes, for blouses and skirts, for materials and patterns. My cutting table and the table for my sewing-machine would both be specially designed. Then at least I might have become tidy. Nothing would be left lying about. In addition to these two large rooms I would have had three small bedrooms, each with a modern bathroom.

But now that the road was to cleave through the mountainous side of the Point, there was no use in dreaming any more.

I would therefore momentarily settle for a tallboy which would stand in a corner of my present room, commensurate, of course, with my own height so that I could delve comfortably into the top drawer without having to stand on my toes. The first drawer would contain make-up and nail varnish, those phials a woman guards as jealously as witches in fairy-tales guarded their love potions and the wax dolls in which they stuck pins. In the second drawer I would put the silk scarves and squares of which I have collected so many during a lifetime that I forget where I have hidden them, and thus invariably wear the same one. The third drawer would be for gloves and accessories, the fourth for bras, the fifth for girdles and pantie-girdles, the sixth for slips and half-slips, the seventh for reels of cotton. My tallboy should be made of walnut or chestnut, and every day I would polish it with beeswax till it shone. I have measured the space for it, lived for an entire day in the dream of possessing it, then suddenly realized that if my house were to be pulled down and we were thrown out into the cold, nothing I owned in the way of furniture would fit in with whatever new place I went to. So I shall not buy a tallboy after all. Most of my wishes end that way.

There is too much uncertainty, too much discouragement, too many expropriations, too many riots. And what am I in all this but a woman who wanted a tallboy?

Although some years ago I reduced the size of my kitchen garden, it is still too large, and every year I find myself racing against time to prepare enough ground for planting and sowing. All down one side of it, parallel to the hedge which in February and March was full of primroses, cowslips, wild violets, periwinkles and wild strawberries, are fully grown cherry trees whose fruit should ripen successively between early June and mid July according to the different species. Under these this year, against the advice of all the experts, I planted potatoes in the hope of cleaning the earth which was getting full of couch-grass. I am told the plants will be all foliage with no potatoes. We shall see.

At the western extremity of the kitchen garden are plum trees whose fruit is generally spoilt in the bud by bullfinches; to the east a curtain of fir trees acts as a frontier between garden and orchard while on the south is the sixteenth-century bakehouse with its three little rooms. The beautiful slated roof has zinc gutters that allow me to keep a vast tank at the back brimful of rain water so that we never run dry for watering. In this part of the garden are the strawberry beds whose Royal Sovereigns give me great joy.

But the fact is that my kitchen garden is too large, and every spring I have the same nightmare, that I shall not be strong enough to accomplish even the bare minimum. In the very centre of the village, only a few yards from the post office, and nearer still to the office of Maître Vincent, the notary, there is a tiny garden, as large as a tablecloth against the back of a house. I follow it season by season with admiration and envy, with a sort of poetic fervour. Not since I was a child in the Midi have I seen such beautiful tomatoes. The rose trees every June vie with the pinks and carnations to blind one with colour. This small paradise belongs to Mme Mandart whose husband, a former locksmith and iron-worker, a craftsman as fine as any in the Middle Ages, made wrought-iron balconies. Some days earlier, passing that way, I stopped to talk to Mme Mandart in her garden.

'I never wanted a larger garden than this one,' she said. 'Having to keep a house spick and span, and doing all the jobs in it that any woman must do, are enough to teach one that every year one is not quite so strong as the year before. The good M. Deshoulles used to prepare the soil for me every winter. A garden as small as this needs plenty of manure and so he used to dig deep trenches and fill them with farm manure.'

'I employed him myself for two or three seasons,' I said. 'He used to do odd jobs for several of us. The last time I saw him was at Montauzan where Patsy Poirot had engaged him to dig the flower beds. She was not at home that day and, as I was walking back along the drive, I saw M. Deshoulles, his chin resting on his hands which were folded over the handle of his spade. "Ah, Mrs Henrey!" he cried, "It's all up with me. I guess I've just worked too hard. The strange thing is that when I'm not working I'm bored to death, and when I start digging or mowing I feel a deathly tiredness stealing over me." Because he was not without a sense of humour he added, laughing. "You caught me taking a nap just now!"'

'As you probably know, he was a master baker,' said Mme Mandart. 'I think he knew pretty well everything there was to be known about bread. When he was a boy they used to knead it with their elbows. Electricity has halved the work, but the bread no longer has the same taste. M. Deshoulles died in the spring and now I can't find anybody willing to put in a day's gardening. They all get too much from the government for doing nothing.'

But though my own kitchen garden, not to speak of the flower

garden, often seemed beyond my strength, what surprised me was
the increasing pleasure that I derived from gardening. My transistor, tuned in to Radio 4 of the B.B.C., brought me successively
news, a play, some Mozart and on Wednesday afternoon the admirable church service that is one of its most precious gifts to
people in faraway places. In the dignity of its religious broadcasts
the B.B.C. is unique, and though the French state radio, on its more
serious wavelength, gives many worth-while talks on an academic
level, its desire to keep Church and State well apart is all too
evident, with the result that there is apt to be an aridity in certain
aspects of everyday life that may well have its bearing on the
unhappiness of its youth.

The student trouble at Nanterre showed no sign of abating,
and now for the first time Paris newspapers were starting to
talk about Trotskyite and Maoist student groups who harboured
not only the Red but also the Black flag.

Nanterre!

What picture does this place-name evoke in my mind? Why of
course. It reminds me of certain Sunday mornings when my father
Émile and I set off hand in hand to look for mushrooms and
tender dandelion leaves along the banks of the Seine between our
flat in Clichy and Nanterre. Yes, Nanterre. All that bend of the
muddy river was rich, marshy land ideal for the market gardener.
My father and I wore our canvas shoes, and he generally wore the
grey cotton suit my mother had made for him. This was the first
time she had tried her hand at making a man's suit, and she
couldn't get over the fact that she had found it much less
difficult than she had imagined. She exclaimed, very proud of
herself: 'And why shouldn't it be easy! No hips, no behind,
no bosom. There's nothing to a man!' Milou, of course, was
tall and spare. Wiry might be the best word, but lithe and
strong as a lion, always a little afraid of his own strength. We
would set out along the Avenue de la République, crossing the
Seine by the Asnières bridge. The muddy water smelt good and
the river was a joy, but scarcely had we crossed it than we came
upon the pestilential smell of a soap and candle works that kept
its distinctive odour in spite of it being Sunday morning and the
factory closed. Soon it cleared and we smelt again the mud of the
river, even when the tide was flowing fast. Only those who have

lived by a river, like the Seine here, or the Thames at Kew, are aware how good a river smells, in spite of factories. To this smell of ooze and slime must be added others, just as fascinating, at least for a little girl out with her father on a Sunday morning: the smell of the cabbages that were planted in long rows like soldiers on parade, thousands of them, all the same shape and size. Then also the lettuces, delicate and refined, sheltering under their glass domes upon which the sun, when it shone, made little beads of perspiration from the dampness inside. The market gardeners, Milou used to tell me with a faint desire to shock, poured the contents of the Paris sewers on this flat ground to enrich it. Was he showing off, I wondered? Ought I to believe him? But how delightful to feel that little tremor of horror running up my spine, for a tale like that was evocative of Émile Zola's most picturesque underworld. We went from one market garden to another, and then across a second bridge, stopping half way across to lean over the parapet and watch the tugs towing their long line of barges, like ducks followed by their young. When a tug came downriver it would let out a long, piercing cry, and a man on the bridge would pull a string and lower the funnel so as to avoid hitting the arch. 'What are they carrying?' I would ask my father, anxious to hear him air his knowledge. 'Paving stones for the Paris streets! Barrels of wine from the Midi! Coal!' We would set off once again and make for Courbevoie and Nanterre.

Nanterre! Yes, I recall the noisy, clattering, narrow-gauge tramway that clanged past a highwall which, my father explained, hid an old people's home or workhouse. Beyond the wall one glimpsed the tops of trees. There, hidden from our sight, lived the inmates whom I imagined as being bent with age, miserable, with nobody left in the world to care about what happened to them. Milou, with his furious love of liberty, was even more terrified than I was of this unseen prison. 'Better to die than to end up in a place like that!' he would say, gripping my hand more tightly and hurrying past.

I am happy to think that he never did grow old but died instead at what should have been the zenith of his strength, like a giant elm that is unsuspectedly hollow. Hard work had exhausted him. He had been sent too young down the mine.

Small cafés, some with arbours, were dotted all along the banks of the Seine, and they smelt of fried potatoes and white wine. The wine was served in tumblers so thick that I used to tell myself as a little girl that they must have been hewn out of a glass paving-stone. But how excellent the wine tasted after the long walk and all the excitement! I have often sought to recover the tang, the coolness, the dryness of the wine we drank on Sunday mornings at Nanterre, but in vain.

I would wait patiently for my father to finish the bottle. He would not have dreamed of leaving it unemptied. Besides, he had paid for it. The wild flowers I had picked along the river bank were beginning to wilt in my arms. I clutched them near to me as a mother clutches her child, pressing it to her breast. But my father had also collected trophies to take home. He used to bring with him an old tin box with holes punched in the lid. This was for the snails he discovered in the course of our walk. He claimed that, though of a different species, they were just as succulent as the ones found in Burgundy. Nobody had such a a gift for preparing them. 'You'll see!' he would say. 'Just wait till I've finished with them!' and he would pour himself out another glass from the bottle. Matilda, my mother, was always horrified when he presented her with his snails. But to me, cooked by my father, they were caviar!

I had not yet seen the new university built over what in my girlhood was low ground rich in mushrooms of the kind we called *bolets*, or boletus, and snails, of the small grey species, and dandelions. But almost every night now on television we were kept just sufficiently abreast of what was happening so that nobody could accuse the government of entirely hushing it up.

The cameras began to acquaint us with blinding new buildings and acres of concrete where boys and girls had cell-like rooms about which there were endless interviews. About the right of girls and boys to mix. About restrictions on their movements. About it being both too far and too near to Paris. About never being treated quite like grown-ups. About the lack of personal contact and sympathy, out of lecture hours, between students and professors. About how much better all this was managed not only at Oxford and Cambridge but also in the United States.

There was also a contributory factor to psychological unrest at Nanterre, the existence not far from the university of a shanty town or *bidonville*, one of those leprous, insanitary conglomerations of tin-roofed huts which continued to lie like open sores round the periphery of Paris, and which housed workers and their families from other lands.

In the course of an interview with a group of students at Nanterre, several of them told us that in order to kill time they went to the Spanish and Portuguese families in the neighbouring *bidonville* to teach the children French without tears.

'When we have taught them to read and write', said these students, 'the children will be better equipped to start school.'

It struck me that this interview revealed a situation almost as explosive as that which from time to time causes race riots in different parts of the globe.

Not more than a few miles away on the other side of the river in the Bois de Boulogne could be seen the lights of those new quite incredibly luxurious apartment houses where there may still be a penthouse flat for sale at something in the region of fifty thousand pounds.

# 5

ON THIS beautiful May morning Georgette arrived to deposit the milk can on my kitchen table.

'Brigitte is on strike!' she exclaimed with a wry smile. 'Oh, not through any fault of her own, the poor innocent child, but what with all this trouble at the Sorbonne, and the General Strike, and the way it all seems to be spreading! Well, we weren't sure, of course, what exactly was happening at the *lycée* at Deauville. In spite of what they told us on television about all the professors and school teachers coming out, or being locked in, it's all so confusing. Jacques and I advised Brigitte to go to the *lycée* as usual and find out for herself. She wouldn't want people to think she was shirking her lessons.'

'That would not be at all like Brigitte,' I agreed.

'No,' said Georgette, 'it certainly wouldn't.

'So she found the *lycée* closed?' I queried, anxious to hear the end of the story. I could not help laughing at the idea of little Brigitte, so often the head girl of her class, being obliged to go on strike like the Maoists at the Sorbonne.

'Well no, not exactly,' said Georgette. 'A few of the pupils had arrived like Brigitte to satisfy their consciences and to see what was happening, and just one or two teachers. The geography teacher, for instance. As everybody stood around, not knowing what to do, the geography teacher gathered the children in a classroom and said: "I see that there is nobody to teach you maths today, but I suggest that rather than let you waste your time I give you a short geography lesson?" Brigitte and some of the other girls sat down and took out their notebooks, but suddenly a gang of older students, mostly sixteen- and seventeen-year-old boys, broke into the classroom and cried: "What's the matter with you kids? You know what happens to little Gaullists?" And the boys made such a din that the geography lesson never got started, and Brigitte came home.'

'A few days' rest won't do her any harm,' I said softly.

'I'm sorry for the parents whose children were to sit for their *baccalauréat* next month,' said Georgette. 'And even for the children, like Brigitte, who have no examinations to pass this summer, it's disturbing. It's so easy for the hot-heads to get at them.'

She paused by the garden gate, and said: 'Your roses are coming along nicely this year.'

'There are years like that,' I said, 'when nature appears to be making a special effort. It reminds me of the summer when Paris fell.'

'As Brigitte won't be going to school for a day or two', said Georgette, 'I may get down to making her the navy blue blazer with the two rows of gold buttons she wants. You can have no idea how precise she is with her instructions. She knows exactly what she wants, and if I didn't obey her to the letter she just wouldn't wear it. She wants it slightly pinched at the waist. "I thought it was the fashion to have them cut straight" I said to her. "That was last year," she said. "This spring all the girls at the *lycée* are wearing them more closely fitted, with short tartan skirts like Scottish kilts."'

The next morning we drove to the small market town of Dozulé to buy ten chicks because none of my hens had been broody, and I was short of cockerels for the late summer. The country lanes were unbelievably beautiful and everything seemed peaceful. The things that most affected the running of a house, like electricity, were just as they always were, though we had been advised to get off as much mail as possible before the sorters in Paris went on strike. On our return, therefore, I spent the afternoon writing urgent letters. Our son was just then in Tokyo on his way back from Melbourne to New York. I hoped I would be able to hear from him before postal deliveries and telephones ceased.

The eight or nine days that separated us from Ascension Day—a national holiday—saw so many things happen quickly that I still feel a little shiver of apprehension. It was not so much what happened as what the things that were taking place might portend. It might take years to know the answer. One evening during the thirties I boarded a German aeroplane in Hamburg

on my way to Berlin. A Nazi S.S. leader with a swastika armband
came up and sat down in the seat beside me. His *Heil Hitler* and
his jackboots froze me into a similar paralysed apprehension.

The rioting in the Latin Quarter, the destruction of budding
chestnut trees with electric saws, the burning of motor-cars, the
looting of shops, the singing of the 'Internationale', the clasped
fists, all froze me. All that was feminine in my nature made me
mortally afraid of what might result from the end of an era.

The making of the navy blue blazer gave Georgette even more
trouble than she had feared.

'I do so hope I have understood exactly what Brigitte wants!'
she confided. 'She is so sweet, so gentle, so affectionate—but oh,
so exacting. She has a picture in her own pretty head of just how
the blazer must look. Last night she said to me: "If you don't
think you can manage it, Mother, I would rather you didn't go
on with it." Would you believe it? But now that I have bought
the material and started to cut it, I just haven't the heart to give
up. I felt a bit discouraged this morning and now it does me good
to talk about it. What are we parents coming to, allowing our
children to frighten us out of our wits! And all those men in the
government giving way all along the line! No newspapers, no
letters, and people filling their jerry cans with petrol in case the
pumps run dry!'

'By the way,' I said, 'one of your cows—I think it was the one
with the white line down her back—made a terrible to-do all
night. What's wrong with her?'

'I know,' said Georgette. 'She's on heat. We'll be coming for
her later.'

Towards ten o'clock I drove down to the village to get the
bread. Mme Eudier, the bakeress, and her husband had driven
back in the early hours from Paris where they had spent the
previous day. 'Oh, the traffic in Paris!' cried Mme Eudier. 'Some
people got stuck in the Place de la Concorde for two hours.
People just park their cars anywhere and the police say nothing.'

But now that the General was back from his triumphant
journey behind the Iron Curtain we all felt that something con-
structive would happen.

Turning in at the white gate I came upon Jacques, M. Levannier and Georgette taking the cow with the white line down her back to the bull. Jacques stopped by the car to bid me good morning.

'The grass looks a lot nicer since we made that arrangement,' I said. We had divided the home orchard in two, keeping the cows or the heifers all day by the river, then allowing them to graze anywhere by night.

'By the way,' he said. 'Have you been to Dives lately. The Red Flag and the emblem of the Viet Cong are flying side by side from the top of the town hall. You should go and see for yourself!'

As it was market day we decided to go to Dives.

This small town is less than twenty minutes by car along the main Deauville–Caen road. We can join it by taking the Chemin du Loup, a short switchback lane which runs between the Michelin estate and one of Mme Bellay's orchards. Rather to our surprise Mme Bellay's washing was as usual hanging on the line outside her farmhouse. Could it be that negotiations were held up by the present upheavals?

There was little traffic on the main road. In a moment or two we were passing the small market garden whose owner had just died. His property had temporarily been withdrawn from sale because of the threat of the new highway which after swallowing up our own house and La Pointe would emerge somewhere here. Another minute or two and on our right was the lane leading to the twelfth-century church of Auberville in whose quiet churchyard my mother is buried. Then on through lovely country and glimpses of the sea to Houlgate where the road takes a sharp left turn to follow the sands to Dives.

The *perception* where we paid our rates and income tax was closed as the staff were on strike. From several windows of the town hall we could see the flags Jacques had talked about. To see the Red Flag hoisted above a factory occupied by strikers had become almost normal. To see it so aggressively displayed from a municipal building showed the gravity of the present bid for power. That the colours of the Viet Cong should hang beside it could, one supposed, be interpreted as an open snub to the United States, like burning the Stars and Stripes. But there had been incidents in Grosvenor Square in London that had been just as provocative, except that they lacked the semi-official character of this one. As for the occasional vaunted emblem of the Chinese Peoples' Republic, this was an echo of what was happening at the Sorbonne and in a score of other universities up and down the land. This was the work of extremists who were reaching beyond conservative Communism to a new and more explosive shockpoint.

Apart from these manifestations that one might easily have missed driving through quickly, how quiet and apparently normal everything was! Thus can one sometimes live through history while scarcely being aware of it. Leaving the main road we parked the car beside the church which in some form had stood here when William set out to conquer England. This coast has the unique distinction of having witnessed two invasions— one that set out to conquer England, the other by the English and Americans to restore France to the French.

M. Dupont's chocolate shop, one window facing the church, the other the narrow street closed to traffic on market days, was crammed with cakes and chocolates made by this celebrated master cook. His chocolates, compared with the price one pays for chocolates in England, were so expensive that I bought them only half dozen or so at a time, thinking myself wildly extravagant. His old mother, gentle of expression and most correctly dressed in black, her grey hair drawn tightly back, was showig an specially made birthday cake to a customer whose perfume, the latest by Guerlain, reminded me that I had first noticed it on Andrée Pradeau.

'Oh, madame,' I exclaimed, 'how good you smell!'

'You are kind to say so!' she said, smiling. 'It does smell good, doesn't it? My son brought it to me on his return from Paris the other day, and though it always takes a little while to blend a new perfume into one's own personality, I am beginning to feel that it has become part of me. The gifts that a mother receives from her son are amongst the most precious, aren't they? I must add that he is the father of the young man whose birthday we are about to celebrate, and for whom M. Dupont has made this magnificent cake with its eighteen candles.'

'You mean that you have a grandson aged eighteen!' I exclaimed, looking at her in admiration. How youthful she looked in her bright red coat and mini-dress in grey jersey.

In the street leading to the covered market, the blind man was

once again playing *Paloma* and, because it was a favourite of
mine, and because he always seemed to be playing it when I
passed, I dropped a coin in his hat. There had been occasions in
history when revolutions were sparked off by famine. The last
time I was struck by such an abundance of fine food was at St
Malo during the summer of 1940 when stragglers of the beaten
French army lay sprawled without discipline or hope on the hot
sands. The shops in the historic town were filled to overflowing
with ribs of beef, entire hams, immense slabs of local butter and
stone jars of fresh cream. How the Germans on arrival must have
gorged themselves! I know they did, because my mother, who
remained behind, saw them do so. Here in this covered market,
structurally unchanged since medieval times, was gathered so
much food that once again I felt a gulp in the throat. Passing
rapidly through it to the open-air market, I stopped in front of
the cheese merchants whose array on long trestled tables under a
huge open-sided tent was one of the most remarkable in the
entire province. No cheese, French, Italian, Swiss, Dutch or
German, was said to be missing, and the men and women
serving all along one side worked with the speed and expert
knowledge that came from having been brought up since childhood in the business. There were two brothers, for instance,
whose dexterity was prodigious, I found them difficult to tell
apart because both resembled the film actor Kurt Jurgens in his
younger days, but the one who generally served me was called
Robert, so I usually waited till somebody called out his name.

For some time now I had noticed that the hitherto unspoilt
country between Houlgate and our own village was showing
signs of the builder. What particularly intrigued me was the
construction of a stadium whose roof was not yet completed,
and I wondered for whom and at whose expense this monstrosity
was being put up.

To my surprise I saw men working on the dome, and this
seemed to prove that the stoppage in the building trade was
not complete. Feeling suddenly brave, I decided to drive in
through the woods.

Parking the car near a clump of trees, I discovered that I had
stumbled on a group of buildings erected in the former grounds
of a millionaire's private estate. Ancient trees, some from the

Far East, rockeries and cascades of limpid water remained witnesses of the past.

As nobody took any notice of me I proceeded through the extensive grounds. A printed notice outside the secretariat building revealed that I was in one of the government's training colleges for students training to be teachers of physical training and sport. I had heard about this place from Georgette. The games master of tomorrow would take his games degree as the science master took his, and the hockey mistress of tomorrow would concentrate on hockey instead of having to study a Latin primer and teach little girls *amo, amas, amat* as she was obliged to do in the old days. I decided to walk a little farther and seek one of them out.

Everything was very clean and modern. The students' quarters gleamed with glass and cement, but the place seemed deserted. On a notice-board in the entrance hall were duplicated notices, student news sheets and manifestos that left me in no doubt about what had happened. The students were all on strike. Those who remained had taken over.

I now felt like an interloper in a ghost town, but decided nevertheless to take the long way round and inspect the playing-fields and the other buildings. In one of them I could see through walls of plate glass some young men in white practising Japanese wrestling, but they turned to look at me and I hurried on.

'Are the students on strike?' I asked two middle-aged men talking outside the secretariat.

'Yes, they are all on strike.'

'What are they striking about?'

One of the men laughed.

'Do any of them know?' he asked. 'But what is on most of their minds, I fancy, is what will happen to them when they are no longer young enough to play the games they will be teaching others to play. Youth doesn't last very long these days.'

'How is modern society going to settle that one for them?' I asked.

The second man shrugged his shoulders.

'They can't have it all ways,' he said. 'Doubtless they'll be retired at forty.'

Next to this group of buildings on land bordering the main

motorway was another of those budding housing estates like the one being developed at the Château de San Carlo, small red-roofed cottages and pseudo-half-timbered walls to give them an old-world atmosphere, but extremely modern with pretty bathrooms and all-electric kitchens, even to smoke disposal units. The houses were individually built to order, but the prices were astronomical. The newly planted lawns between cottages were subject to rigid regulations. One tended to be luxuriously imprisoned within an expensive fairyland.

Were these the sort of houses in which superannuated games masters would retire at forty, wondering what to do with the rest of their lives?

Because her parents were unable to leave Paris, where events were becoming increasingly serious, Laurence Pradeau, whose lectures were suspended in Paris for as long as the Sorbonne was occupied, stayed alone with her Irish setter Loïca at 'Bois Lurette'. Thinking she might be nervous alone in the big house I invited her to stay with us while things continued to be difficult, but she refused, saying that with her gun and her dog she felt perfectly safe. She did, however, consent to lunch with us.

The first gooseberries were ripening in the kitchen garden. On the day she came I resolved to give her a real English meal, a sirloin from one of our neighbouring farms, followed by gooseberry tart and cream. Nobody in France ate gooseberries, which were to be found neither in shops nor on market stalls. In spite of the prevalent snobbishness amongst so many people for drinking whisky and making use, often inaccurately, of English words and expressions, many of the most succulent dishes that make English cooking so excellent were either scoffed at or utterly unknown. I had told Laurence in advance what to expect, and she was delighted. Her enthusiasm was just what I had expected. She was that sort of girl.

I never tired of admiring her intelligent features and slender body, for it was as if nature had wanted to make her perfect. Her wide shoulders, narrow hips and long, beautifully shaped legs made her move with rhythm and grace. She used practically no make-up, her skin having the natural quality of dark ivory, setting off admirably her large dark eyes and blonde hair. She was essentially a country girl, devoted to all the activities one associates with English life in the shires. Doubtless because of this she had a serene and unruffled disposition. On her father's side she came from a long line of relatives who were distinguished in medicine and surgery (on her mother's side also for that matter), and after lunch she told us how she had been present at a heart operation an uncle of hers carried out on a little girl who would otherwise have died. 'When the surgeon's knife pierced that tender flesh I held my breath and nearly fainted,' she said, 'but afterwards everything went with such speed, precision and assurance that I was overcome by admiration.'

We talked about the coming marriage of her sister Danièle to a young executive of an international oil company. The wedding originally planned to take place at 'Bois Lurette' at the end of June might now have to take place in Paris instead. Things were so unsettled that one could not reasonably ask guests to absent themselves for a week-end in the country. There was no public transport in Paris and nobody could tell if things would get better or worse during the weeks to come. Danièle herself, who was private secretary to a famous Paris barrister, had to walk to and from his chambers every day, and as the Pradeaus lived at Neuilly this was quite a distance.

'You had all worked so hard embellishing 'Bois Lurette' for the wedding reception!' I exclaimed. 'How disappointed you must be?'

'Yes,' answered Laurence, 'I had been looking forward to a real country wedding.'

We had now been three weeks without newspapers or mail. Newspapers were published in Paris, but were prevented from reaching us because of a strike among the distributors. The telephone continued to function until pickets were placed outside the telephone exchange at Deauville, after which only emergency calls could be accepted. Radio and television became the centre of a bitter struggle, the details of which were to a great extent hidden from the public. Newsmen urgently desired freedom from government interference in the preparation and dissemination of news. They claimed that they were being made merely the mouthpiece for government propaganda. News must be free and unshackled, was their cry. This, according to the minister responsible, was not possible. Parliament had put radio and television in shackles; only parliament could remove them. Meanwhile fourteen thousand men and women in radio and television, irrespective of their political beliefs, remained adamantly on strike. On the whole their grievances sounded better founded than the grievances of all the others put together. Who would deny that in a free world news must remain free? Who could tell but that this had been the basic reason for everything that had taken place? Freedom of thought has always been more worth fighting for than freedom to make money.

The absence of the usual television programmes suited me personally rather well. At 8 p.m., after being treated to a short summary of news, we were given an out-of-date film and sent to bed. So to bed one went rather earlier than usual, and with the luxury of listening peacefully to the B.B.C.'s 11 p.m. news.

The next time Laurence came to lunch she had one of those violent colds that one gets at her age. She had gone down to the sands and bathed, and then been chilled by a bitter north wind driving across from the English coast. A lot of young people who would normally have been at the university were staying in the country till the troubles were over, and they used to descend in their fast cars on Laurence while she was in her potting sheds or finishing the now unnecessary decorations in the big house, and lead her off on their various expeditions.

I wondered what they thought about the events that were taking place all about them, these young people whose financial expectations, perhaps because death duties in France between parents and children were almost non-existent, allowed them to live relatively favoured lives. Most of them had jobs waiting for them. This was one of the chief bones of contention among students, who complained that both at the university and afterwards the sons of the professional and executive classes were favoured at the expense of those whose parents were manual workers. Had the government made too many reforms, rather than too few? Paul Gaxotte, an eminent historian and member of the French Academy, was to write in the *Figaro*: 'Everything was done to push thousands of boys and girls into the universities who, because their true vocations lay elsewhere, and they possessed other capacities, had no business to be there. By acting in this manner we rendered them a disservice, condemning a number of these young people to face life with neither a valid diploma nor a learnt trade.' The fear of being sent down, of not passing their finals, doubtless prompted a vociferous minority to urge that all examinations should be abolished both before reaching the university and on leaving it. We had really reached the *Alice in Wonderland* stage.

One night the television news had been particularly depressing —a police officer rammed in the stomach with an iron bar, trees sawn down with the ubiquitous electric saw, a young man stabbed to death, paving stones hurled from barricades of over-turned motor-cars, a police inspector killed in the provinces by a lorry whose brakes had been released by strikers and war memorials to the dead of the 1914–18 war daubed with insults. After watching all this I had a mad, absurd dream. I dreamt that all the dead members of my family had been resuscitated and were joined by those still living to form a community in a dream village.

Down this village street walked a soldier, my maternal grand-father, the Zouave. He would protect us. My grandmother had been a washerwoman and so she, in my dream village, continued to wash the linen. My paternal grandfather was a schoolmaster who would carry on his useful occupation while my cousin Nègre, a priest in a tiny village in the Auvergne, would take over the church. Cousin Nègre, a dark little man with a rich accent, had met my father and me when I was a very little girl and we had travelled all night on the hard seat of a third-class railway com-partment to go and stay with him. Wearing his poor shiny cassock, he took me up in his arms and kissed me, saying to my father: 'So this is your little girl, Émile!' My father's grandfather who had been a beadle, a violent man but imposing in his Swiss Guard uniform, would be useful to cousin Nègre in his church. My father Milou could either build houses or work in the mine, if there was a mine. My mother Matilda would be the local dress-maker or perhaps found a factory of ready-to-wear clothes which would amuse her enormously, while her sister Marie-Thérèse, so pretty, so dainty and such a gifted *modiste*, could make all the girls in the village wear hats again. Her husband, butler to a millionaire during his lifetime, could keep the hotel. My cousin Rolande, who had married a baker, would bake our bread while my other cousin, Jean-le-Bodo, whose father had sold books to

Anatole France at Tours, would be in his bookshop of rare books. His wife Fernande had once kept a stall of second-hand books on the quays of the Seine in Paris. Their elder son Christian was one of those C.R.S. (phonetically Ceres) mobile police who sped alongside the President of the Republic on motor-cycles, the second son was editor of the *TV Times* and the third son was a press photographer. All these found their place in my village.

# 6

THE very important man in French industry was standing at the corner of his hayfield watching the machine cutting the hay with its giant arms. His two youngest children were perched beside the farmer on top of the machine, and there was a smile of contentment on the business man's face because he was where he liked best to be, and the sun was shining. I had turned the small car into the drive to call on his wife. It was the third Sunday in June and, as the situation all over the country was slowly improving, I guessed that the family might be here for the week-end. To my surprise the man's wife did not come out of the big house to greet me.

As I drew up on the gravel path the husband walked slowly over the verge of the hayfield—large, important, smoking a cigar and still smiling. I think he was pleased to see me. He said:

'How nice of you to come over. My wife and daughter have gone to call on friends, but they will be back soon. Will you stay to lunch?'

I said that I had guests of my own, but that I would call back during the afternoon before they drove back to Paris.

'You must have had a very anxious time,' I said to him.

What a beautiful morning! All the flowers in the garden, the roses, the sweet peas, the honeysuckle, the peonies, the carnations and the pinks were filling the warm air with their scent and mixing their perfume with the sweet smell of the newly cut hay. The cherry trees were laden. Never had we known such a year for cherries. Why, normally the birds ate all the early cherries and we never had a look-in till the late ones ripened in mid July, but this year the birds just could not deal with them all, and the early trees remained laden. What a summer for strawberries too!

The children's laughter echoed across to us from the hayfield. The man said in a low, almost detached, voice:

'My opinion is clear and precise. We have just lived through the end of the capitalist system as we know it in France. A month ago I thought it might drag on for another twenty years. Now everything is changed. I give it less than ten. What has been happening in this country is something so tremendous that it marks the end of an epoch. Its repercussions are bound to be felt before long in other countries where people may still believe themselves immune.'

'Were your factories occupied?'

'No, but this had nothing to do with the wages we paid our employees or whether they were satisfied with us or not. They received orders from their unions to remain at work. The plan did not include any witholding of food from the population.'

'Why did it have to last so long? Couldn't the General have acted more quickly?'

'He may have relied a fraction too long on the magic of his personality, but when things got worse he needed to make sure of the army. That is why he went off on that secret journey. He gained his vote of confidence from the army, of course, but on certain conditions, one of which was the immediate release of army chiefs implicated in the Algerian conflict. As soon as he was back in Paris the capital was surrounded by tanks. I saw them myself. This doesn't mean that an army, however loyal, can be expected to clamp down on nine million workers. It merely means that on this occasion a show of force sufficed.'

'And now?'

'I am tempted to answer that what happens now is immaterial. The workers have witnessed the might of their own power. They will demand, and be given, half of all the profits their company makes. If there are no profits, or if they appear insufficient, they will sack the chairman and put somebody in his place of their own choice.'

'It sounds pretty tough on the shareholders!' I said, laughing.

'One suspects that the shareholders saw the writing on the wall', said the great man, 'when the rioters marched to the Bourse the other day and set it on fire. Wasn't that clear enough?'

'You haven't mentioned the student riots?'

The man became serious again.

'Our own sons and daughters are as closely involved in what the students are asking for as the sons and daughters of the

working classes. If you are a Protestant and you send your child
to a Roman Catholic school, the chances are ten to one that he
or she will become before long a Roman Catholic. Or, of course,
vice versa. When we send our children to colleges and universities
where nearly all the teachers and professors are either extreme
left wing or avowed Communists, as they are in France, don't
be surprised if they learn at the feet of their masters. People like
myself must learn to live with this. The teacher makes the future
man almost more than the parents.'

He puffed at his cigar, looking thoughtfully at a squirrel
running across the lawn.

'The teachers or professors have troubles of their own of
course. They are being overtaken in progressive thought by
their own pupils. Doesn't history teach us that this nearly always
happens? For instance, a university professor in France kept his
professorship in principle till he reached the age of seventy. He
was supposed to grow wiser as he grew older. Undergraduates
now claim the right to sack any professor who has ceased to give
them satisfaction. They point out, with some reason, that a teacher
in scientific subjects is no longer abreast of new inventions
after the age of forty. So why not off with his head!'

'Yes,' I said, 'I heard a famous Paris surgeon saying just that
the other day on television.'

After lunch I went back to see his charming wife and daughter,
and we had a delightful visit in which all three of us relaxed with
feminine chatter. We mentioned neither strikes nor politics, none
of us women being quite certain whether the 'revolution', as
everybody called it, would mark a point in history, or whether
in a few weeks' time it would all be forgotten like a piece of
bravado in a musical comedy. There was nothing much that we
could do about it anyway, except to worry about the children,
about the men, about our homes.

The boys and girls went back to college, and every evening
Brigitte, on her return to Berlequet, regaled Georgette with the
news of the day. And Georgette passed it on to me.

'She puts things in a more colourful way than they do in the
newspapers,' said Georgette admiringly. 'She makes me *understand*
things.'

'Oh?'

'About relations between teachers and pupils, for instance. That is one of the problems there has been such a fuss about it, isn't it?'

'I gather so.'

'One of the teachers, very sure of himself, decided in the new spirit of Marxist equality to ask his pupils what, if anything, they found to criticize in his work and behaviour. The teachers themselves, he said, had not failed in their duty to point out the shortcomings of the Ministry of Education. He was now with equal frankness asking his pupils to say what they didn't like about him. Well, for a few moments, Brigitte said, nobody dared speak up. They thought it must be one of those jokes that inevitably end in the discomfiture of the boy or girl rash enough to fall into the trap. But at last a boy (for no girl would have dared say such a thing) put up his hand and said: "Please, sir, what we don't like about you is that when you have set us a problem to do you sit back in your chair, put your feet up on the desk and smoke a cigarette. It's not respectful." '

The teacher, according to Brigitte, and as Georgette recounted it to me, was not pleased, but, trying not to appear uncomfortable, asked nervously: 'Anything else?'

'Yes,' answered another boy. 'We don't like your mannerism.'

'My mannerism?'

'You keep on stroking your beard. It gets on our nerves.'

'I appear to be full of faults. What else?'

'The way you punish us by making the boys walk on all fours between the desks. That's not dignified for children of our age.'

This story, according to Georgette, had a sequel. The teacher arrived in class next day with his hair cut short and with no beard. He was also a model of politeness. 'It's a funny sort of revolution,' she added thoughtfully. 'They all talk their heads off, but for the first time those who talked louder than the others appear to have been beaten at their own game.'

Nevertheless neither she nor Jacques appeared quite as serene as they were six weeks ago. The brutality of events shocked them. They found it hard to comprehend the mentality of some of the older boys at the *lycée* at Deauville who had gone to a timber merchants during the height of the student riots, threatening to burn the place down if the men employed there did not strike.

They were frightened by the sight of the Red Flag on the town hall at Dives and frightened by a paragraph in a local newspaper telling of rioters who killed a cow in calf and cut up the carcass. On that occasion Georgette and I were no longer owner and tenant but sisters under the skin. In the minds of the extremists the farmer, whether tenant or otherwise, had become the hated reactionary whose presence would not be tolerated in a Maoist regime. I recalled the resentment in Georgette's voice when she told me about the strikers at a certain factory. In order to swell their funds, they went round with a collecting box to the farms in the plains of Caen. When the busy farmers suggested that these vigorous young men should do a day's work on the land by helping them to thin out and replant the young beetroot plants, they became abusive and insulted the farmers. This was perhaps the first time that all our tenant farmers in the region suddenly realized that the workers numbered them among the bourgeoisie.

Though everything appeared to be momentarily reverting to normal, my own special problem remained unsolved. The General would have his majority, but the shadow of the road still hung menacingly over my house. Fear came back to me worse than ever. In a real revolution we might all have gone down together. It is comforting perhaps to know that others are suffering at the same time. In the present circumstances I felt that I was the only one to pay.

Perhaps not the only one. Georgette was no happier about the road than I was. My house would be engulfed. My family and I would be thrown out into the cold. But the house that Jacques and Georgette lived in would be shaken by the bulldozers. The cattle would take fright. The quiet orchards would become dusty, noisy and unhealthy. In due course thousands of cars would be roaring by day and night.

I worried too much. I tried to do too many things. Men can relax more easily than women. The house, the garden, cooking the meals, washing the linen, stealing an occasional moment to jot something down on paper: the feminine round is interminable. I would revolt. I would take a day off. I would not write a line. Not answer a letter. Not even run to the telephone if it rang.

At seven I went down to the kitchen as usual where the Aga was not at its warmest, its most comforting red self, because the flues needed cleaning. The three cats were mewing at the door. The cock was crowing in the stables, impatient to lead the hens out. Because of the sultry weather there were flying ants on the kitchen floor.

The cats had been out all night. All three were born hunters, but when they were not hunting they slept either on the wood pile behind the stables or in a soft lined basket on the deep stone ledge outside my study window. As soon as I opened the door they would rush in, arching their backs against my legs, demanding the great bowl of warm bread and milk that I gave them every morning. A similar breakfast, hot bread and milk, went to the birds who had a platform in front of a birdhouse opposite the kitchen window, arranged in such a way that we could see them while having our meals. Even the jays, usually so fearful, came for their breakfast. Meanwhile the cocks and hens were rampaging in what used to be a corner of the stables but which I had now made over to them. They needed their mixture of corn and wheat, and sometimes a hot meal, before going off to join the cows in the orchard. The chicks would have bread and milk like the cats and the birds.

With a kettle of rain water on the Aga, every time I passed through the kitchen I would drop boiling water on the percolator for our coffee. I used rain water in preference to well water for making tea, coffee and cooking vegetables because it was soft, brought out the flavour of tea and coffee and left no rims on the stainless steel pans when we cooked vegetables.

Breakfast was the most exquisite moment of the day. Night was behind me. I was a coward at night. When just after midnight I felt finally obliged to turn off the bedside lamp and try to sleep, I experienced moments of veritable anguish, exactly as if death stood beside me waiting. I could hear my heart beating violently. Pain that was bearable by day became unbearable by night. The stillness of the orchard through the open window, with only the occasional moan of a cow, the hooting of an owl, the call of a nightjar, terrified me to the point of panic. My mind was peopled with phantoms of regret and disappointment, remorse for the past, fear of what might happen if ever I was left in the hands of strangers in a strange land. Fear of growing old made me angry, unjust, rebellious. My happiness died at night, but I was reborn every morning to the light of the garden and the smell of coffee on the Aga. But after breakfast, while opening the top of the Aga to put the anthracite in, I decided to clean the flues, although it was my day off. The Aga was the heart of the house, that kept it warm and alive all through the night and the day. When, on very rare occasions, it needed attention, I gave it the priority one gives to a sick child. I had an old pair of black cotton stockings which I kept specially for the operation, using them as long-sleeved gloves so that, protected from the tips of my fingers to the shoulder-blade, I could plunge into the opening at the back of the chimney and remove any of the very fine soot that might have accumulated there. Before I had learnt to do this I used to telephone every six months to the agents at Caen who would tell me to allow the Aga to die down. The firm would then send two men in a lorry to do the job, leaving my kitchen in such a state that it took me half a day to clean up the mess. In addition, of course, the operation cost me nearly a week's house-keeping money.

Left to myself, I could do the whole thing in twenty minutes, fill the Aga with its morning ration of coal and get straight on with my ironing. I have a horror of workmen in the house. Their boots fill the place with mud, and a smell of stale tobacco is apt to linger over the next meal. Today all went to my satis-faction, except that in going to fetch a spoon from the silver drawer to scoop up some soot at the end of the flue I forgot that I had my gloves on, with the result that I scattered soot all over the silver.

As the sun was shining, and the garden at this early hour was as pretty as a dream, I decided to take a chair out on the terrace and clean the silver. It needed doing anyway, as it had been on my list of things to be done for some weeks.

For I have a list. Mistress of my destiny, I have learnt to give myself orders. I decide what needs doing and write it down. For instance,

> Sow the parsley
> Buy corn for the hens.
> Wash jersey skirt and pullovers
> Cut a blouse
> Mend a slip

Sew on a button
Clean the silver
Knit a sleeveless pullover
Also another with sleeves

At the end of the day, before listening to the 8 p.m. news on French television, I took a blue pencil and crossed out all the things on my list which I had successfully accomplished during the last twenty-four hours. By writing these items down I had the impression of lifting them above the state of feminine futility. I made them important. Such is the power of the written word.

As soon as I was comfortably seated on the red-brick terrace with the tray of silver, some polish and a chamois-leather, the cats arrived from nowhere. Their constant desire for human companionship was such that if I walked to the white gates at the top of the orchard they would immediately frolic round me. Often, in order to show off, they would race away to one side and then, swift as lightning, climb up an apple tree, looking down at me triumphantly from a high branch. In the afternoon, when I planted a row of young cabbages, the three cats would similarly arrive from nowhere and remain with me all the time. All three were females—the grandmother, the mother and the daughter. I had kept the youngest because she was black, black as a witch, and I hoped she would bring me luck. But all she brought me was news of the road.

I washed the forks and spoons, and some flat Georgian candlesticks which we used during power failures, in warm, soapy water, admiring their brightness. Now they looked so nice that I would have to change the flowers in the big room. The rain water tank in the garden was brimming over with the night's downpour, and this reminded me that I ought to fetch a basinful to wash the pullovers and jersey skirt that figured on my list of things to do.

Soon after eleven, with the woollies washed and rinsed out in rain water till it ran cool and clear, I went off into the kitchen garden to cut a salad for lunch. My lettuces were coming along nicely. I might even dig up a few new potatoes. Though my morning walks through the kitchen garden were always filled with good intentions, there was so much to inspect and to admire that I often ended by forgetting why I had come. The two quinces on the quince tree against the half-timbered wall of the bakery were now as large as walnuts, and as it was the first time in my life that I had ever grown quinces I was madly excited, planning to make jam with them in October. The night's rain had brought on a new crop of strawberries and soon, forgetting everything else, I had gathered four or five pounds of Royal Sovereigns for jam making. I never made more than ten or twelve pots of jam at a time. I found that I could watch it better.

Lunch was over and the silver and crockery put away. The cats were asleep on the couch in my study. The kitchen was fragrant with the delicious smell of strawberries simmering in the big stainless steel pan on the Aga. As it was my day off I would read the papers quietly in my room. We were only just beginning to receive the backlog of over three weeks' accumulated mail, an occasional letter dated a month earlier. Some of it, I reflected, might never reach us. The mail was always a problem. When there was not a strike in France there was one in England. It was like those public holidays which never happened on the same days in New York, London or Paris, so that when one was disposed of another cropped up.

I had just started to rest when I heard the tinkle of the bell on the garden gate and in came the three little Mainier girls. I had rashly promised one day to give them English lessons. The Mainiers were coal and grain merchants. The twins, Marie-Laure and Marie-Claude, celebrated their First Communion on the same day as Brigitte. Their tent for the festivities had been erected in the coal yard, and was so large that it covered it completely. The supplies of Russian anthracite had been allowed to run out in advance, so that the yard could be broomed and scrubbed and, as in the case of Brigitte, the rejoicings had gone on for three days and three nights.

The twins had brought with them their youngest sister Mireille, who was seven. These English lessons were apt to prove frustrating affairs, because the mothers were so much keener on them than their daughters. When some mother said to me,' Could you possibly help my daughter with her English, Mrs Henrey?' I never had the heart to say no. Naïvely I imagined that the girl wanted to learn English so that later she could speak and write it well enough to become a bilingual private secretary in Paris.

But of course that was just an absurd dream. All the girls really wanted was just enough to scrape through an examination, after which, goodbye to all that! None of them had the insatiable ambitions that I generously lent them in my more fanciful moments. It hurt me to see a girl wasting her opportunities when my imagination persuaded me that in her place and with her youth I could accomplish so much.

Using shock tactics, I set up Baby Mireille in front of us as if she had been a rag doll. Pointing to her ears, to her mouth, to her nose, to her cheeks, we repeated each word in French and English. We said: 'Her eyes are blue!' 'Her hair is short!' 'Her lips are pink!' 'Her name is Mireille.' 'She is seven years old!'

'Now,' I said to the twins. 'Supposing you repeat what we have just learnt?'

But the twins looked at each other and pulled terrible faces. They creased their foreheads and opened their mouths wide, but no sound emerged. Then they shrugged their shoulders and gave up.

No wonder Brigitte's teacher makes his pupils walk between the desks on all fours, I thought. But at least a schoolmistress gets paid for her trouble. Instead of my pupils being allowed to make such scant use of me I would make use of them. I would delve inquisitively into their little feminine minds. Abandoning English, I asked Mireille in French:

'Do you like going to school, Mireille?'

Our little seven-year-old pouted: 'Not much.'

'Have you any girl friends?'

'Yes,' she answered, without enthusiasm.

'Have you a boy friend?'

Smiling archly, and with no sign of embarrassment, she answered. 'Of course!'

'Do I know him?'

'Naturally.'

This was getting exciting.

'Does he live far from your place?'

'He lives opposite.'

Opposite? Well, what exactly was opposite the coal yard? Nothing, except perhaps the notary's house, but all the boys there were too old for little Mireille. Feeling like a new recruit in a parlour game, I said aloud:

'The house most nearly opposite yours in the main street is the notary's house.'

Baby Mireille's cheeks were flushed with pleasurable excitement. She was playing with me. She had me at the end of a string. She said: 'No, not the notary's house. Try again.'

The twins were gurgling with laughter. It was the first time I had seen them break out of their bored insensibility. I swiftly took advantage of this exceptional atmosphere, to announce.

'Amoureux in English is *sweetheart.*'

The twins, nudging each other, bubbling over with gaiety, repeated: 'Sweetheart.'

Baby Mireille, anxious to keep up the suspense, burst out: 'You haven't guessed right yet!'

'No,' I answered. 'I give it up.'

'It's François Levallois!' she cried.

'Good heavens! I never thought of him.'

François was the nephew of Mme Baudon who kept the grocery store.

'Naturally,' said Baby Mireille, 'we are in the same class but he's much more intelligent than I am.'

'Naturally,' I said, 'boys are.'

This remark not generally accepted allowed me to ask the twins if they also had boy friends. They made the most extraordinary faces, blushing violently, and obliging me to use a great many artifices to edge them on. At last one of them confessed that her boy friend lived at Trouville. Having revealed this important information, she assumed the voice of a grown woman, to continue:

'So we can't meet on Sundays or during the holidays. It's a nuisance because I'm so afraid that during the summer vacation he may forget me.'

'Or you forget him?' I queried.

'Oh, no!' she cried. 'Never!'

'What about you?' I asked the other twin.

The other twin confessed that her boy friend was a grandson of old Mme Dière who, when I first bought my house, lived in one of her own, as old and as beautiful as mine, and as she had a garden she sold lettuces and such like from a laden basket on market days. One day, when she and I and her daughter Jacqueline were gossiping, the little boy in question made off with my bicycle and was soon careering through the streets of the village on it. As his legs were too short to reach the pedals he looked like a contortionist on a trick bicycle.

'My goodness!' I said to the twin. 'I bet your boy friend leads you a dance!'

'You're right!' she exclaimed. 'He's the life and soul of the school bus. I'm lucky to have him!'

'Well,' I said, 'that's all for our English lesson today!'

I had invited Monique Bessel, daughter of Mme Bessel, my tenant farmers' milkmaid, to come to tea, and scarcely had the three little Mainier girls disappeared giggling over the brow of the orchard than I saw Monique's tall figure through the open window. Gone once again was the quiet repose of my hoped-for day off.

Monique's mother, whom at one time we used to call (because it was such a pretty name) La Julienne, was one of those country-women chiselled out of all that is most robust in nature. She was plump rather than tall, dressed in black with her hair in a tight, neat bun, and worked uncomplainingly from early milking time till dusk. She was the sort of countrywoman who bore the heat of the sun as stoically as the downpour, supporting a husband, rather than being supported by him, carrying on her broad shoulders all the four walls of the house. She and her husband had worked for Mme Anger, a tyrannical widowed landowner, whose rich orchards, bordering my own, stretched away into the near distance. When I was young in these parts I used to see Mme Anger driving down to the village in her buggy to sell milk. Her forceful character made her feared rather than loved, and I think she died more or less alone in her large, cold house which for me at least had always had an air of mystery about it.

After her death the land was cut up, and my son bought one of the orchards, not the largest, but one of the prettiest and most lush and useful because it ran down to what we called my small wood, to differentiate it from the triangular one near the Burgundy—a small wood in which there were several dozen large oaks, watered by a stream.

The Bessels' house and garden formed part of the orchard my son purchased from Mme Anger's estate. There was some arrange-ment between my tenant farmers and Mme Bessel whereby she

milked their cows morning and evening, and looked after their
place when they were away, while in return the farmers paid her
rent and gave her a small wage.

When I drove down to the village every morning to buy
newspapers and bread, to post the mail and collect what was
waiting for us, I occasionally saw Mme Bessel walking down under
the trees in Cathedral Lane, clutching her two black cloth bags
which she would soon fill with her morning's shopping. I would
stop the car and open the door so that she could ride down with
me, but I was never quite sure if she did not really prefer to walk.
She used to get so stiff sitting every morning on her three-legged
stool milking some fourteen cows that her body needed the
rhythm of the long walk to and from the village. When I did
pick her up the drive was so short that our conversation was
limited to news about her children. She had just married off her
son to a girl from a neighbouring town and we stopped for a
moment so that she could show me the photographs.

'Ah!' I exclaimed, 'and there is your daughter Monique who
was training to become a hospital nurse.'

'Oh, but she is one!' cried Mme Bessel, showing sudden
pride. 'She has passed all her examinations and is now a fully
fledged nurse. I am expecting her home tonight for a fortnight's
leave.'

'Then ask her to come and have tea with me,' I said. 'I would
love to see her again.'

So here was Monique in mustard-coloured stretch pants, tall,
much thinner, elegant and very much at ease with a becoming
hair style. Her features were round and her large blue eyes
prominent.

'I hear that you did very well in your examinations,' I said.
'We are all proud of you.'

The compliment made her blush, tempering her assurance with
a delightfully feminine modesty. To this was added the softness
and charm of her voice which she had inherited from her mother,
who invariably rounded up her cows in a voice so warm and
musical that I never knew her to have the slightest trouble with
them, not even with the difficult animals on stormy nights when
they were nervous and on the rampage.

'It wasn't always easy,' Monique was saying, 'but fortunately
Mother was determined that I should have a profession, and not

have to do what she does. Not that she is ashamed of milking the farmer's cows. Far from it! And not that I lack affection for them. I love the cows. I was brought up on a farm, wasn't I? Do you remember when I was little and sat between the milk churns? But Mother has had a terribly hard life. She still has. A girl today must do what she can to take advantage of what the world has to offer. I think I was always ambitious. In fact I am so ambitious that I am surprised when I don't find the same ambition in other girls of my age. I worked hard, but on the other hand I consider myself fortunate. I attend the senior surgeon in our operating theatre. Even at the beginning I never fainted or made a fool of myself. What worried me was the fear of picking up the wrong instrument or not guessing immediately what he wanted. Instruments look so different when they are all laid out in a theatre than when one is studying them in diagram form in a textbook. Those were real moments of panic.'

'Was that the most difficult part?'

'No, what was most difficult was the time before I was a nurse— the sticking to my courses at Trouville, wanting to do something so much that I could force myself in the depths of winter to go alone from the mud of our little house, under the dripping trees of Cathedral Lane and down to the village to take the bus. And at night coming back all alone while the owls hooted. That's not always easy for a girl. My father thought it would be enough for me to learn how to keep house. I could have stayed in bed in the morning.'

'Do you find things changed?'

'They have changed and I have changed. I'm more under-standing and less frightened of things that move in the dark. I hate to see the beautiful chestnut trees in the Chemin de San Carlo being cut down. It's the same in the little market town where I'm working now. But, as I didn't know it ten years ago, I don't mind so much. Our hospital is modern and well equipped and I love my work, but I am increasingly aware that I lack the culture that some other girls have and which I must acquire by my own efforts if I am to make a complete woman of myself. So in the evening I try to read a lot. Books of literary merit, I mean. But after a day's nursing, with all the books and papers one has to read anyway to keep abreast of one's profession, it needs the same sort of determination to improve one's mind as it needed to set out from our muddy house to catch a bus on a dark, rainy morning. Am I boring you?'

'Far from it.'

'To give you an example, it was after a hectic day and I had gone to my room to lie down and rest my feet. They give us special shoes to wear in the wards. They are a big help. But oh, how tired one's feet can get by the end of a day! I had my transistor on. I didn't like the music it was playing much, but I was too tired to change to another station, so I let it run on though, frankly it got on my nerves. However, I closed my eyes and relaxed, and little by little I actually began liking the music they were playing and trying to understand it. That's when the miracle happened. I was quite transformed by the end of the piece. The announcer said that it was Ravel's *Bolero*. I had the impression of having just been introduced to somebody who would become very important in my life. I wanted desperately to know more about Ravel!'

Monique blushed.

'I couldn't tell that to anybody else, not even to Mother. I thought you might be different. That you might understand.'

'I do understand.'

She hesitated.

'I said just now that I had changed. When I was first in the wards so many things came to me as a surprise—not medical things but things about people. Things that have made me more understanding. One morning we admitted a very old lady, very gentle, very patient, but quite abandoned by the world. I took a liking to her and did my best to make her comfortable, but after a day or two she said to me: "Nurse, don't get yourself overtired on account of me. Just do what you are paid to do, nothing more. I don't want to get better. My family has ceased to love me. I am old and have become a nuisance. The kindest thing both for them and for me is to let me die quietly in my bed." "Rubbish!" I exclaimed gently. "You are overtired. I'm going to see that you get a nice rest." But the old lady was right. Though there was nothing physically wrong with her she had discovered that she was unwanted, and so very quietly she allowed herself to die. I thought this only happened in novels, that nobody any longer died of a broken heart. In hospital the things one laughed at suddenly assume a tragic reality.'

'Are the patients nice to you?'

'Some are but others are not. Many of them are only just emerging from their peasant state, with the result that one is shocked in these beautiful new hospitals, so white and clean, to find the majority of patients frankly dirty, with the kind of disdain for hygiene that I have learnt from my midnight reading to associate with characters out of Balzac and Zola. How does one equate this old-fashioned lack of cleanliness with colour television and rockets to the moon? I am very careful when suggesting to a patient that it might be nice for him to take a bath, but often his susceptibilities are such that I end by insisting that it is part of the treatment and vital if he wants to get well.'

'Tell me about young women in these small towns. Do they talk about the Pill?'

'They talk about it, but most of them are too frightened of what it might do to them to take it. So girls of the bourgeoisie are apt to come in with miscarriages which fortunately, because of antibiotics, can be dealt with quickly and efficiently. Girls from farming communities, on the other hand, are far too scared of pain to attempt a miscarriage. They come into the maternity wards and make arrangements for their children to be adopted. What is strange about these girls from the small farms is that they are tough when it comes to long hours and hard work, but cowards when it comes to physical pain. Whereas the opposite often applies to girls of higher education.'

Most of the nurses in her hospital, she said, were older than she was. In fact she was the baby, but this did not prevent her having many friends of her own age. They went to the theatre at Caen. The shops were very fine and there was the Faculty of Medicine.

Did she think she would end by marrying a doctor? Well, it was still too early to tell.

# THE 'LITTLE DARLINGS' AND A
## SMART WEDDING

## 7

DANIÈLE PRADEAU was not to have a country wedding after all. Too many of the invited guests were unwilling to absent themselves from Paris during elections which already, to the immense relief of nervous citizens, promised to give new life to a régime so gravely menaced by the 'revolution' of May. The date Danièle had chosen would remain as before, the last Saturday in June, but instead of taking place in our village church the marriage would be solemnized at St Jean le Baptiste at Neuilly, the elegant suburb where the Pradeaus had their Paris apartment. During the afternoon there would be a reception at the Tir aux Pigeons, a club amidst lawns and beautiful trees in the Bois de Boulogne.

With the business of the country virtually back to normal and the government so certain of re-election, victory was in the air. Mme Eudier, the pretty bakeress, beamed at her customers from behind tall wicker baskets full of freshly baked loaves. Her joy at this early Gaullist landslide reflected the sentiments of our peace-loving village. All we needed now was to see our announcer friends back on television, but they were still engaged in a stubborn battle for freedom from government control in the presentation of news, a cause that meant very little to a nation burning to get away with its children for summer holidays.

There was also Nanterre, the university where the trouble had started more than a year ago, the last Easter but one to be exact. Lionel Hanrard, our local garage owner, who was so good-looking, a man of perpetual good humour, had a brother who lived at Nanterre, and, when I asked him to look my small car over so that it wouldn't let me down on my long journey to Neuilly to attend Danièle's wedding, he exclaimed, *à propos* of nothing: 'By the way the boys and girls are still occupying Nanterre University. Why don't you stop off there on your way

to Paris? It played a role even more vital than the Sorbonne or
the Odéon in the events of May. My brother would show you
over only, as it happens, he also is getting married. Any of the
girl students would take you round.'

'I could leave a day earlier,' I said. 'At dawn, for instance, on
Friday to be at the university at ten.'

'After Mantes', he said, 'and Flins, where all that rioting took
place when police evicted the workers from the Renault factory
on 6th June, there is a sign on the *autoroute* telling you where to
branch off for St Germain. From St Germain it is a straight run to
Nanterre.'

I would go to Nanterre. I would walk again hand in hand with
my mother through the streets of Clichy. I would make a pilgrim-
age to the church of St Vincent de Paul where my parents were
married. I know because I attended the wedding!

'What a good idea,' I said to Lionel Hanrard. 'I'll leave in the
morning.'

Paris is 126 miles from our village. The best way is through
Deauville. It was planned in due course to link Deauville with
Paris by an ultra-modern speedroad with two or three lanes in
each direction, often at different levels, so that the through journey
could be accomplished in a fast car in an hour and a half. Exactly
half this tremendous undertaking was already finished, the
sixty-five-odd miles from Evreux to the St Cloud bridge in Paris.
Here one can travel at the speed of an express train, often faster,
for most people do eighty miles an hour. The Deauville end was
under construction. At Touques the road divided, one side going
to Trouville, the other to Deauville. It was from Touques that a
lateral road was planned that would swallow up my farm.

I set off on my great adventure just as it was beginning to get
light on that Friday morning, just as Mme Bessel was softly
calling the cows, driving them to the top of the orchard where
she would milk them.

Would the weather be fine? For the first twenty miles low
clouds over this enchanting countryside gave me the impression
that it might rain, as it had done on the previous day, but beyond
Lisieux the sun came out in an explosion of heat, and I suddenly
knew that I had brought all the wrong clothes, a Chanel two-
piece and a small fur cape for the church, instead of a light

summer dress which I now longed for. Why had I not thought
of this before? As usual I had been more concerned about the
animals I was leaving behind than about my own needs. Georgette
had promised to look in every morning and evening, to fill the
Aga, feed the cats and the hens, give bread and milk to the chicks
and look after the birds in the garden, but she and Jacques were
haymaking in the Burgundy this week-end. They would have their
hands full.

I saw the first poppies, blood red splashes, on waste ground
near Mantes as the car droned on and the needle of the speedo-
meter remained steady at sixty, and I became aware, as I never
had been before, of the proximity of the Renault factory at
Flins, scene of recent violence. The hitherto almost unknown
place name had acquired the sort of overnight notoriety that the
village of Waterloo must have acquired in the eyes of passing
drovers after the battle. One's senses took poignant note of it as
the car flashed past. Everything was over now, the factory had
presumably become normal again, but would the bloodshed and
the hatred evaporate as completely as a bad dream when morning
comes? Would the Communists forgive the Gaullists for their
increasingly massive victory?

Now here was the road sign warning me that I must leave the
highway and proceed in the direction of St Germain, to which the
French Court hurried during that other unsuccessful revolution
known as the Fronde. At three o'clock on a cold January morning
in 1649 the eleven-year-old Louis XIV, the future Sun King, was
pulled half asleep out of his bed at the Palais Royal in Paris, on
the order of his mother Ann of Austria and her Minister Mazarin,
and driven through the dark streets and lonely roads to this
château which loomed ahead of me. How familiar in retrospect it
all sounds—even the reason for calling that particular revolution
the Fronde because students in Paris used at that time to amuse
themselves by catapulting stones from the ditches at the police!
The previous summer there had been three days of fierce street
fighting in Paris, from 26th to 28th August 1648 when students
and others under the leadership of agitators built barricades with
empty wine barrels, upturned carts, broken furniture, tree trunks
and iron bars, from behind which they hurled whatever came handy
at the officers of the law. No wonder there grew up in the youthful
king such an aversion for the turbulence and revolutionary

spirit of Parisians that he eventually built his royal residences of modern design at Marly and Versailles.

Because Friday is market day at St Germain, and it was difficult to pass through the centre of the town instead of taking the more direct road to Nanterre by Le Vésinet, I followed the southern loop of the Seine past luxurious new apartment houses with flowered terraces and roof gardens, past enchanting glimpses of river, river tugs and towpath, past Marly where water was pumped for the Sun King's Versailles, past Louveciennes where the unfortunate Mme du Barry was arrested, past Malmaison where the Emperor Napoleon visited the Empress Josephine, and then to the Place de la Boule, the heart of Nanterre. What a lot of French history to digest on the way, guessed rather than glimpsed between factories, some prosaic, others making world-renowned perfumes which romantically we dream about.

Now the very name of the avenue we followed, the Avenue F. and I. Joliot Curie, warned that futility and royal fairy-tales were behind us. Here was nothing beautiful, nothing to save us from the curious aridity of morning sun, of harsh light on rubble and cement; a narrow bridge over a railway line, a suburban station with an electric train drawn up at the platform, the name of the station incongruously La Folie, a tree-lined street giving unexpected prettiness and shade along the track, and two girls walking briskly along in the direction of an open gate.

I stopped the car and asked them: 'Where is the university?'

Vaguely surprised, they answered: 'Through the gate.'

'Can anybody drive in?'

'There's nothing to stop you.'

'I rather wanted to find some young women undergraduates to tell me what it has felt like to be at Nanterre all these long weeks. The papers say that the "revolution" started here, that one hundred and fifty students brought the whole scholastic edifice of the nation tumbling down, and that it was they who sparked off the industrial strikes—over ten million people laying down tools, occupying the factories, dictating terms to the government. I would like to find out what it felt like during this long time to be partly responsible for such a to-do. You both look so innocent in your gay pullovers and mini-skirts!'

They laughed.

'I take it you are both undergraduates?'

'Oh, yes, we are undergraduates, but you would do better to go to Block C and inquire on the fourth floor. The girls there may be able to help you.'

They stood for a moment facing me on the path beside the railway line, so young, so fresh, so pretty in their bright, simple clothes. I ought to stay here and make them talk, I reflected, but for some curious reason they frightened me. Their faces, faces of young women on the threshold of life, were both childish and serious. One did not picture students like these hurling stones.

I got back into the car and drove through the open gate and along a rough road leading between waste ground, overgrown with hemlock, thistles and glorious wild poppies, to an open space between the long university building, with its ugly square towers and a relatively low edifice facing it which contained an immense modern swimming-pool. Here I parked the car and made my way towards the faculty building.

Every block was entered through glass doors. On each side of the doors the outside walls had been daubed with sayings of Mao Tse-tung in crimson paint, which here and there had run. Thus against the wall of this particular block was scrawled in giant letters:

> The masses alone are the motive force, the creators
> of universal history.

Beside it a student had conjugated the verb 'participate', the watchword of the newly announced Gaullist philosophy of financial partnership between industry and its employees:

> I participate
> You participate
> He participates
> They reap the profit!

Well, this at least was what I had come to see for myself, an adoption of something beyond Marxism, the teaching of Mao Tse-tung, and side by side with it some gentle lampooning of the Gaullist regime. Let us now push through the glass swing doors and penetrate farther into the temple of youth! Shall we be shocked or disappointed to find only platitudes?

Everything is still clearly photographed in my mind.

Ahead of me was a wall on which was an electric clock whose hands pointed to ten o'clock. What admirable time I had made on the road! On either side of the wall were corridors leading to the interior of the building, the one on the right blocked by two girls sitting on the floor amongst piles of current bourgeois magazines and periodicals, such as *Elle* and *Marie-Claire* and *Femmes D'Aujourd'hui*, which seemed to prove that even the most progressive girls are at heart like the rest of us, romantic sentimentalists and furiously attached to the idea that our salvation lies in marriage and home. I took it that the girls in the middle of these periodicals were not there to read them but to sell them. I merely noted the conservatism of their wares.

The wall in front of me was covered with slogans and posters and some rough lettering under the clock:

What must you do to discover if a young person is a revolutionary or not? What is the distinction? There is only one rule. Does this young person wish to identify himself with the mass of workers and peasants —and does he, in fact, already do so?   Mao Tse-Tung.

All this I took in at first glance. But something else, by some failure of my optic lens, did not penetrate for another brief moment of time. Yet it was the largest and most obvious, the most terrifying in its undertones of anarchy, and I who am not easily shocked was left staring at it like some poor innocent beast in front of the raised fang of a poisonous snake.

The poster depicted Hitler as I had seen him a thousand times on posters, newspapers, magazines, during those nightmare years between his rise to power and the fall of France. Hitler with his familiar wisp of dark hair, his mad, convulsive eyes, his little moustache, the famous Nazi shirt and tie, the swastika armband, Hitler who filled us with panic and fear. Well, here he was, and I had seen him so often that I fancy this was why I saw the poster without it registering at first. But here was the difference. Hitler, just as we had known him, was holding out in his right hand a mask of General de Gaulle!

Slightly sickened, I turned into the left-hand passage on whose dirty walls were scribbled slogans and insults in pencil or pen.

'If you see a wounded C.R.S., finish him off!'

This passage opened out on to a very wide corridor, like the covered deck of a monster liner, running the entire length of all the faculty buildings and lit from the low ceiling. You could pace up and down this deck, as indeed scores of youths and girls did, addressing friends, leaving them to speak to others, walking slowly and meditatively, reciting lines from Marx or Freud or some fragment of a soliloquy from *Hamlet*, or running along distributing leaflets, inviting students to vote on a certain motion or to attend a protest meeting.

On one side of the long deck were painted futurist designs and so many sayings, quotations or lampoons in French, English, Chinese or Arabic, that one could have spent an entire day deciphering them. A poster echoed the government's interference with radio and television, itself a government body known by its initials O.R.T.F. (Office of Radio and Television of France):

> The Police Talk to You
> Every night on
> O.R.T.F.

Or these words maliciously ascribed to the much maligned General de Gaulle:

> Do please leave me in power
> for another 10 years!

The paintings on the wall produce a strange, macabre effect, less by what they depict, which is unintelligible, unless they have a hidden meaning, but by their colouring, sombre reds, midnight blues, deep yellows, all applied in varying thicknesses as if with a scrubbing brush or an old-fashioned witch's broom. The overlaid writings are made with lipstick, eye liners or coloured chalks. The weirdest sensations overcome me. At one moment I have the impression of having been catapulted into a space world of a kind quite different from anything found on earth; at other moments I cannot resist trying to compare this stark university building with the one I saw in Moscow, but of course there is no comparison possible, for in Moscow no lone, inquiring woman like myself would be allowed to wander unescorted through passages, up and down stairs, in search of what is hidden behind these inflammable words and pictures, which in their turn would not be allowed to exist. Imagine a student of foreign extraction trying to paint arabesques on the walls of the Kremlin! No, this is a world of fantasy of a kind that has never existed before. I am glad to be seeing it now and not as it will be in six months time or in a year when its historical undertone shave been erased by fresh paint and buckets of detergent. I am breathing a period of history as fascinating therefore as the revolution of 1848 which Flaubert described in *l'Education Sentimentale*:

Michel-Evariste-Népomucène Vincent, ex-professor, emits the desire that European democracy should adopt a single language. One could make use of a dead language, for example, a perfectionised form of latin.
'No! Not latin!'

I am absolutely fascinated by the youthfulness, the prettiness, the cleanliness of the girls who swing past me in their vivid pullovers and mini-skirts, with bright smiles and complete detachment from the more indecent outpourings on walls and stairs. They look like flowers daintily overstepping an ocean of broken glass, remnant of some philosophical battle. Many of the youths are bearded, but I find them immensely obliging when I approach them with a rather timid request for information. One of them offers to break off from the business of distributing leaflets to act as my guide, but when I politely decline, asking instead to be shown where the girls are working, he takes me to the foot of the stairs and points helpfully upwards.

I pause on the hard, cement stairs to read the inscriptions on the walls. What days, weeks and months of incessant scribbling! Shall I find a Montaigne, a Rousseau, a budding Voltaire? Here is something so cruel that I wince. Once more it concerns the leader of the nation. Not about him but by him. My cheeks burn with sorrow for him and resentment for this is what I read:

> 'One must not allow great men to grow old
> in the exercise of their power.'
>
> Charles de Gaulle during the trial
> of Marshal Pétain.

Was it for this that he gave these boys and girls the money and the opportunity to be educated at a new university? To bite the hand that was lifting them out of the proletariat to make intellectuals of them? Would he not be read about in history books by future generations long after these youngsters had ceased to be undistinguished school teachers or obscure village notaries?

On the first landing some boys and girls were squatting on

camp stools. I asked questions. Nobody seemed surprised. Everybody asked questions. Everybody had a right to speak. They thought about my problems for a while, then pointed to a room, the door of which was open. 'Try in there!' they said. So I went in.

The room was a corner room with lovely windows on two sides that flooded it with morning light and brilliant sun. By one of the windows, sitting at a desk, was a young man, pleasant but rather unkempt as if he had not slept in a proper bed for a long time. He was engaged in desultory dialogue with a group of friends. My arrival interested him and he bade me take a chair. Then, calling his companions to witness, he explained that he had been a student here virtually from the time Nanterre began to function. He said that it was indeed a fact that to Nanterre fell the honour of having started the 'revolution'. 'But to be precise,' he explained, 'the movement dates back to the Easter term of last year when we men students occupied the girls' living quarters.'

'Why did you do that?'

'We did it because of the absurdity of a rule that the girls could visit the boys in their rooms, but that the boys could not go to the girls. We considered that the authorities were treating us like schoolboys—not by the standard of university life.'

'So you occupied the girls' building?'

'Yes, for about a fortnight, the last ten days of the Easter term and the first days of the vacation. The idea of occupying the girls' living quarters made sensational headlines in the press. We had more publicity than we expected. In fact there was a great deal more to it than that. We wanted political freedom and some sort of participation in the running of the university.'

'What do you mean by political freedom?'

'To have our own political societies, much as they have at Oxford and Cambridge, and to have free debating societies and to write articles and pamphlets.'

While the young man was talking a slight commotion was taking place in the rest of the room, and I suddenly became aware that one or two men, older than the others, had approached us and were looking at me. I asked rather nervously:

'Is it because I have no right to ask questions? Perhaps I should not be here at all?'

'No,' said the young man. 'They don't mind you being here. You can stay if you like.'

'Well, what's it all about? Is it a political meeting?'

'Good heavens, no. They are a couple of dons looking for a quiet place to give those students a *viva voce*.'

'You mean that in the middle of all this scholastic life is going on?'

'Well, it is and it isn't. The undergraduates are occupying the university, but we are quite happy to have the dons about and, as you have probably read in the papers, though the written parts of some of the exams have been cancelled this summer, the *viva* part goes on.'

'We can't stay here,' I exclaimed, 'it isn't fair.'

'Gathering information?' asked one of the dons jovially, looking at me.

'Yes,' I admitted, feeling slightly embarrassed. 'For something I was going to write in English.'

'I hope you won't be muzzled!' he said, smiling.

'I don't think so,' I said smugly. 'The written word in England is still pretty free.'

He grabbed the back of a chair and made off to the far corner of the room where an undergraduate was waiting for him. My informants rose at this point, and one of them said: 'Let us move to an adjoining room.'

The other room was larger with wide windows overlooking the future campus. The exterior of the bathing-pool was blinding cement with a modernistic overlay of metal in Oxford blue. The residential quarters could be seen in the distance to the left and there was another faculty building, for the sciences, I fancy. One saw a lot of rubble, a cement mixer, some workmen throwing broken wood on a bonfire, undergraduates arriving or leaving in small cars, a good many girls in twos or threes whose laughter came up to us through the open windows. My eyes searched out the surrounding country in the vain hope of seeing towers or spires, green meadows and a river like the Isis. The skyline was pockmarked by those appalling modern French tenement houses known as H.L.M. (flats at moderate rentals), tall, unaesthetic skyscrapers that increasingly rob the countryside of its natural beauty. Here, around the campus, were no trees, no shade, no grass for the poetic soul, no church spire or dome, no cool cloister to give repose to the mind, no concession by the state in its fierce determination to wipe out every memory of those far-off days when Church and Government grew side by side, and when monasteries were places of learning and dotted the land.

Three mattresses were ranged side by side by the door.

'Is this where you sleep?'

'Yes,' he said.

These youths were not particularly well groomed, but the girls were bright and spotless, and if they were that way, I reflected, it must surely be because there were boys about. The tables were packed with roneoed sheets.

'May I look?'

'We have no secrets,' he said.

I read: 'CONSTITUTION—Project D. In view of the hurried character of consultations relative to projects for a Constitution, and the fact that these have not been studied sufficiently seriously by the Faculty as a whole, it is thought indispensable to postpone the vote on the new Constitution until the beginning of next term.' 'My! My!' I exclaimed, taking a long breath. 'This budding Jean Jacques Rousseau would do well to simplify his prose.'

'Do you consider that the phrase is a trifle involved?' he asked.

His features assumed such a look of anxiety that I would have liked to reassure him but instead, on a sudden impulse, I got up and said: 'The girls I talked to in the road suggested I should see some of their colleagues on the fourth floor.'

There followed handshakes all round.

Here I was back on the hard cement stairs with a fresh eruption of *graffiti* in various characters and tongues, some linking philosophical quotations to pornographic drawings that were repulsive enough to make me blush, others (because at heart I am no prude and inquisitiveness compelled a continuance of my search) were not without a certain wit. An unknown hand, for instance, had written *à propos* of M. Pompidou, the Prime Minister:

> Beware of
> PompIDOLATRY!

This made me laugh, for at least it showed a certain originality, and it was therefore with a smiling countenance that I entered the room facing the top of the stairs where a number of students sat or lolled on uncomfortable unmatching chairs. Not one looked up at my entry. They all had in common their extreme youth and an air of mental and physical abandon. From time to time one of them would throw out with studied laziness a word or a phrase in the hope that it would inspire somebody else (after a due pause) to do likewise. The room, like the one below, had a few mattresses scattered about. The girls peered into space through curtains of dark hair which, on occasion, they would draw apart with a slow, measured motion of both hands. The boys smoked nervously and looked ill-fed as if they badly needed to be mothered. I had sought out the Ladies shortly after my arrival where I found myself in front of the mirror beside a girl who was painting her eyes. Their reflection stared at me from a pale face framed with the prevailing curtains of straight hair. The place was surprisingly clean, but I was shocked to discover only cold water in the taps. I had the same feeling when, looking in through the great glass windows at the magnificent swimming-pool opposite, I had seen a notice declaring that it was closed.

A gradual disappointment was stealing over me, that there seemed to be so little of the sacred fire which in the past inspired great movements. If one accepted the fact that the scribbling on the walls was the equivalent of political and philosophical broadsheets, one regretted that so much of it represented known quotations from the writings of famous men, from Freud to Mao, from Voltaire to Karl Marx, so little from inspired and turbulent youth. I had small faith in the occasional airy remarks of the boys sprawled on chairs in this room into which I had wandered. With its leader flown away, was this the aftermath of a revolution that had failed? One felt sorry for the girls that their idols had feet of clay.

Looking into another room I saw a middle-aged woman behind a typewriter. The room was full of typewritten sheets of different colours. The woman was copying something from a notebook, and it probably had something to do with examinations because she was spelling out each word aloud, typing it letter by letter, to be sure she got it right. Perhaps they were technical words. I told her that I had broken the point of my pencil. Was there a pencil sharpener in the room?

'Oh no,' she answered. 'I don't think such a thing exists, but I could lend you a penknife.'

She left her typewriter and searched in her handbag, pulling out of it a very small penknife, the sort a middle-aged woman would own. Her presence in the midst of so much youth made me suppose rightly that she was an employee of the faculty, a part-time stenographer who lived in the town. While I sharpened my pencil, I asked her rather diffidently what she thought about the writing on the walls.

'I see nothing,' she said. 'As far as I am concerned those horrors might as well not exist. I am paid to come here.'

I made my way thoughtfully down into the hall again. In front of an ill-lit cafeteria, whose slot machines were empty of food and whose small tables were covered with dirty cups and empty glasses, a group of students was discussing a rumour that the university was about to be closed, by order of the dean. The swing in favour of the government, expected to reach landslide proportions the following day, and the fact that many students themselves were dreaming of holidays by the sea, lent strength to the arm of authority. But youth, quite apart from the factory workers who in certain respects had refused to follow its lead, felt let down. They who had begun the movement of 22nd March winced under the sting of a mission unfulfilled. As a giant poster, put up that same morning, declared in red letters against a white background: 'This is but the beginning of a long battle!'

I picked a thistle in front of the swimming-pool and took off my pullover. How hot it was! I would remain in a light blouse. A girl passed along the side of the road. An undergraduate driving his car stopped beside her. He put his head out of the window. They talked for a moment, and then kissed. Thus love, for the time being at any rate, triumphed over the scars of this unhappy university.

I drove slowly to the gate where poppies painted the sort of picture one associates with the French Impressionists. They are almost my favourite flowers, these wild, delicate things, so intense as they wave their little heads in a summer breeze. But here, within these walls, were they symbols of peace and plenty, as I had seen them in the cornfields of my girlhood, or did they fore-tell a recurrence of rioting and bloodshed?

Crossing the little railway bridge I came to the intersection of two avenues. The sun by now (it was midday) was intolerably hot. Facing me on the other side of the road was something that made me feel quite sick. I stopped the car and sought the shade of a small tree in the hope that I would not faint. This utter degradation in front of me, this appalling stench, was the famous *bidonville* or shanty town! North Africans, Portuguese, Spaniards, all human beings like myself, lived in this human quagmire in which no peasant would even put his pig! If it resembled in some respects an African *suk*, yet the comparison is unfair. Any Arab market place so bereft of the elemental requisites of human life would not be tolerated.

I debated with myself for a moment whether I should walk across the road and approach it or not. I longed to run away, to head immediately for Clichy and the suburban squalor of my girlhood, rather than to face this shameful scab on the fair face of this lovely and proud land. But in all such decisions I have schooled myself to do what I fear to do. If girls and boys from Nanterre came to give French lessons to Spanish and Portuguese children in this disgusting mound, then I would go, even if my presence was resented.

Viewed from where I stood the *bidonville* did indeed give the impression of a mountain of curiously shaped erections of dull red colour. A track, separated from the avenue by a conglomeration of filth and refuse several feet high, ran up the side of the *bidonville*. Leaving my car where it stood under the small tree I walked up this track and at the top came to a fountain in front of which stood three or four olive-skinned children, while an older girl filled a pitcher. A tall Arab strolled up wearing one of those woollen bonnets of coloured criss-cross design after the manner of Kenyatta. He stood in the foreground as in a film, with the city of squalid huts and half-naked children stretched away behind him. There were two or three shops with pieces of meat hanging outside, and vegetables in baskets on the ground, and a café where some men were seated drinking what might well have been green tea. A rat scurried away between two empty tins.

There was no point in my remaining any longer. I had seen what had to be seen, and in a way I felt better. I kept on thinking about the undergraduates who, like the monks of ancient times, were proud to come and teach among the poor and the oppressed. They were the generation who would sweep this mess away.

There was a quotation from Goethe that flashed across my mind: 'I have no fear for the French. They have risen to such heights in the history of the world that nobody will ever be able to imprison their minds.'

What was good in Nanterre would triumph. What was ill would disappear.

So I resumed my journey in the direction of Clichy.

When I look at it on the map the distance is not great. But all is now a vast industrial suburb, and the very idea of walking with my father, my hand in his, between market gardens in search of mushrooms and snails makes me smile. On this occasion the problem was not to lose myself between La Garenne-Colombes and the Asnières bridge over the Seine, and what a problem it was! At some spot I could never find again I came upon a pretty market with an absolute riot of summer fruit in osier baskets—strawberries, peaches, cherries—and I nearly overran a traffic light. I fancy that in my efforts to stop I must have cut in on a small lorry. We looked at each other, and then smiled.

'I'm lost!' I said, 'I'm looking for the Asnières bridge.'

'Follow me,' said the lorry-driver. 'I'll take you right there.'

I have heard it said a hundred times that when a small motor-car like mine bearing a provincial number plate arrives like a country bumpkin in the big city, Parisian drivers invariably make sport of it. In France a motor-car's number plate reveals its origin. People can tell at a glance where one comes from. Calvados, for example, is 14. Everybody, everywhere, knows therefore that I hail from the land of cider apples and Camembert cheese.

But let nobody ever tell me again that there are no Sir Galahads on the road to Asnières bridge! My ideal, courtly knight raced ahead of me, stopping every fifty yards or so to make sure I was behind him. Of course as I was not nearly fast enough and people would cut in between us, unaware of the game we were playing and as, worst of all, there were traffic lights that suddenly turned red on me, losing me a full precious minute, there were occasions when he had to park at the side of the road in the most congested areas and wait for me. Then off we would go again! When finally the bridge was in sight my lorry-driver slowed up, allowed me to come abreast of him and then, with a wave of his hand, turned off in another direction. This kindness gave me a great glow of happiness. I knew that everything would go well for the rest of the day.

The sight of the fast-flowing river and the tall leafy trees on the island site on our left was balm to my eyes. I crossed the bridge, turned sharp left along the towpath and then everything came back to me! I was a little girl again and Matilda, my mother, was leaning over the parapet, enjoying the cool freshness of the water while a light breeze played in her golden hair. An American soldier wearing a boy scout hat strolled over and spoke to her. It was the summer of 1918. The soldier explained that he was in billets at Dijon, which he pronounced Didgeon, and because of this my mother could not make head nor tail of what he was saying. The soldier unbuttoned a pocket in his tunic and taking out a pencil and smiling broadly wrote on the white stone of the parapet the word Dijon.

'Oh,' cried Matilda in her sweet, high voice, 'Dijon!'

'No,' said the soldier, convinced she had misread, 'Didgeon!'

'Dijon!' my mother insisted.

Then we all three laughed. As we stood there, my beautiful mother, with her golden hair and narrow waist, the American soldier, freshly shaved and tall and blue-eyed, and myself, very intrigued, very thrilled, what did we see but a large rat emerging from behind the trunk of a tree, one of those immense elms whose roots stretched down into the cool water. As we looked down at it, the rat ran about between the grass and the osiers of the mud-bank and then dived into the river. As it swam away I remember watching with fascination the wake it left behind it, growing wider till it disappeared. Looking up shyly at my mother, I thought her the most beautiful creature on earth, the creamy whiteness of her elegant neck made more dazzling by the fiery red of her hair and the severe black of her dress. 'Oh,' I thought in sudden panic, 'what if this American soldier takes her away from me!'

A few moments later I was in a Clichy that I did not at once recognize. The tramways had gone of course. Then suddenly there was the statue of St Vincent de Paul outside his church, and opposite him the market where we used to do our shopping. I must stop! I must find a place to park the car, but the traffic roared down the avenue and cars were parked all along the sides of it. There was a magnificent town hall with a garden in front, obviously new and more in keeping with the importance of the growing suburb. But here, unchanged, was the tall grey building in which with a crowd of other girls I had followed those courses to turn us into stenographers and shorthand typists. I had, of course, overshot my mark by now and had to turn the car round and leave it in some convenient corner while I explored all this on foot. My reactions are invariably too slow. I could never reach those high speeds on the typewriter that some girls manage. My shorthand left much to be desired. I drive a car slowly. I swim slowly. I take things in at a flash, but the execution is laborious. I knit slowly. I sew excellently, but after what years of application at my mother's knee, being taught to make clothes for my dolls. Sometimes I dream that I am in an office poring over a notebook, trying to read back my shorthand. The hands of the clock point to 5 p.m. The boss is waiting to sign his letters, and I have not yet managed to type out a single one of them. I panic. There is nothing left for me but to rush out into the street and look for another job.

The car was now nosing among other cars in the beflowered square in front of the new town hall, but there was no room. Very politely I sought the help of a uniformed porter. I told him that my parents had been married at the church of St Vincent de Paul and could he suggest what I could do with my car while I went in. With a pretence at being gruff he told me to get back into the car and follow him round to a secret place where he would keep his eye on it for me while I was away. When this operation had been successfully completed I set off immediately for the church.

How enchanting those rare moments when one can rediscover the sensations of one's girlhood! On Saturdays after leaving the secretarial school some of the girls and I would watch the newly married couples leaving the town hall. The bride and the groom and the wedding guests would climb into horse-drawn charabancs to be driven off to the wedding feast. These charabancs—we used to call them *tapissières*—were open on all sides and covered only by a light roof supported by four rods to which were tied white bouquets and long white ribbons that floated gaily in the summer breeze. The coachman who wore a white cockade in his cap would crack his whip which had a white ribbon tied to the top, and away they would go to the Bois de Boulogne where the wedding breakfast would be held. As there were no sides to these charabancs we girls used particularly to look out for the bride's little feet shod in white satin! What dreams these white weddings evoked in me! On occasion they were not without humour. When, for instance, the groom had drunk too much he might try to climb into the wrong charabanc or even try to kiss the wrong bride, and then what howls of friendly laughter!

I pause for a moment to admire the statue of St Vincent de Paul in front of his church. How touching the tall figure of this man holding a foundling in his cape, another by the hand.

Two churches form this single edifice. The larger of the two is relatively new, or at least rebuilt in the nineteenth century. What struck me about it was the way the chancel had been modernized, with the Communion table and semicircular choir stalls made of roughly hewn blue granite from Brittany. The effect was so bleak that one had the curious impression of coming upon an evocation of Stonehenge. It was easier to imagine Druids than choirboys sitting on these horny pieces. Above swung a chandelier of futurist design, composed of interwoven metal crosses climbing skywards in a spiral. The screen at the back of the chancel was of flaming red plastic.

On the left by a chantry one descended into the original church.

In 1612, when Shakespeare was already rich and famous, and one year before the Globe Theatre in Southwark was burned during a performance of *Henry VIII*, St Vincent de Paul, aged thirty-three, became *curé* of Clichy. This was his church and doubtless it had changed but little. Here he remained for thirteen years, and here, nearly three centuries later, my parents, Émile and Matilda, accompanied by my very small self aged two, came to have their religious wedding.

Now that I was grown up, kneeling in a pew, the late June sun shining through an open door revealing a glimpse of bright flowers in a garden, my mind recalled the strange story.

My cousin Eugène Nègre, brother of that Cousin Nègre, priest of a tiny village of Auvergne, who met my father and me after our all-night journey to pay him a short visit, kept what was known as a *bougna* in Montmartre next to the house where my parents lodged at the time of my birth. These *bougnas* (from the word *charbougna*) were a common sight between the Sacré-Cœur

and the Bateau-Lavoir when Picasso was in his twenties and working there. In them the Auvergnat traders who spoke their own
patois sold coal, charcoal and firewood dipped in resin. They
often, as in Cousin Nègre's case, comprised as well a small, dark
café and an hotel whose rooms were rented by the hour.

This Cousin Nègre was a pious man, eternally unhappy at the
thought that my parents' civil marriage had not been followed
by a religious ceremony in church. He was always telling them
that unless they did something about it they would go from
misfortune to misfortune, and in addition they would forfeit the
affection of his brother, the priest in Auvergne.

My father, who hailed from a part of France as warm as that
of Cousin Nègre, and with whom he could converse in semi-
patois, getting somewhat perturbed about how things were
going, began to be influenced by the cousin's arguments. The
cousin was a tenacious man, and Émile did not desire to be burnt
in hell.

Cousin Nègre's *bougna* was a pleasant place to visit, and
my father had an appreciative eye for the cellar where barrels of a
very good wine from the Auvergne, chosen no doubt by Cousin
Nègre, the priest, were ranged side by side on their little wooden
supports under the old beams. The bouquet of the wine, added
to the smell of the faggots and the edible chestnuts that also
came in sacks from the Auvergne, delighted him. My father used
to say that Cousin Nègre could make money out of a stone, and
that whereas he (Cousin Nègre) had found the cobbled streets
of Montmartre paved with gold, he (my father) had found
nothing but misery and sweat.

Some people who came to the café made rather pointed jokes
about the hotel rooms that Cousin Nègre rented by the hour, but
Cousin Nègre just went on rinsing glasses under the tap behind
his zinc counter and said nothing.

Then it was that my parents lost my small brother from
malnutrition when put out with a wet nurse at Soissons. After
the funeral they took the train back to Paris, my mother clutching
to her heart a parcel containing her child's baby clothes. They
had neither the time nor money to visit me, who had also been
put out with a nurse in the country, for my mother had been
obliged to borrow some money for the coffin. Cousin Nègre's
dire prophecies were beginning to be realized.

Cousin Nègre himself continued to prosper until one day he fell in love. The girl he fell in love with was just the sort of girl he should never have looked at. She was far too pretty, far too fond of dancing, far too enamoured of money. Worst of all she had come several times with different men to his hotel. That in itself should have been sufficient warning, but the devil was in him and he began to look out for her next coming, and soon, in spite of the fact that he was nearing forty, he could not sleep for the thought of her. He told himself that if he married her perhaps she would reform.

When I was about two years old my parents left Montmartre for Clichy, which was just beyond the city walls. The rents were cheaper, the air purer and beyond our newly built apartment house there was a garden full of lilac in which birds sang. Cousin Nègre, still determined to persuade his dear Milou to solemnize his marriage in a church, came to visit us every Sunday, and as both he and my mother were too heartbroken over the loss of their son to make any further objection, arrangements were made for the religious ceremony to take place at our parish church of St Vincent de Paul. Cousin Nègre was best man, and I was brought along because my mother was afraid of leaving me alone in the apartment.

I looked up from the pew where I had been kneeling deep in thought. Gone were the actors in this pathetic drama; Milou, the strong, the hot-head, sleeping in the cemetery at Clichy, my lovely mother in the Norman cemetery at Auberville. Hot tears ran down my cheeks. The verger to whom I had spoken in the larger church, gathering that I was no idle visitor, had gone to fetch the lady secretary and now both of them were waiting for me by the garden door. I rose, the ghosts of the past fading away, and walked towards them. The presbytery garden was just as it might have been in the days of St Vincent de Paul with a lilac tree in the centre, a canary in a golden cage, a parterre of roses, geraniums against the walls and a laundry whose half timbering must have been more than three centuries old. Magnificent trees spread their shade and softened the roar of distant traffic.

Cousin Nègre, as stubborn in love as he had been in his desire to see my parents celebrate their wedding in a church, ended by marrying this girl who never ceased to ply her shameful commerce. She had started her career in a house of ill repute and was not of a kind to be reformed by marriage. Cousin Nègre sold his *bougna* and the small hotel in Montmartre and took his wayward wife to the Auvergne, where in due course she presented him with a daughter. 'I am mad with delight!' Cousin Nègre wrote to Milou, but his wife soon tired of village life in the Auvergne and went back to Paris, leaving her daughter with Cousin Nègre.

My parents and Cousin Nègre exchanged greetings every New Year's Day. The writing of these letters was for Milou a matter of considerable ceremony. When the kitchen table had been cleared he would produce a newly purchased bottle of violet ink, one of those tiny square bottles whose corked top was covered by dark ceiling-wax which required breaking with the point of a knife. Milou wrote a large, slanted hand, holding the paper a good distance away from him because he was long-sighted. He read aloud as he wrote. His letter began: 'My good, old friend.' Its general tenor was to the effect that 'Matalida is well, the little one is growing taller and sweeter and is doing well at school. Work is becoming increasingly difficult to find. How beautiful it must be in the Auvergne. How I long for the sun. We kiss you, Milou.'

After my father's death, Cousin Nègre wrote to us for the last time. He was anxious to know whether Milou had received the Last Sacraments, and added: 'I will have a special Mass said for him but alas it will not be by my dear brother because he also has gone to heaven.' He added this pathetic postscript: 'My daughter is turning out just like her mother. I have a heavy cross to bear.'

I have no doubt that he also is now in heaven.

The lady secretary had been telling me about the granite altar, the chandelier and the red screen in the larger church. She was anxious to explain that everything had its significance. She had the sweet voice peculiar to spinsters, for, if my theory is correct, spinsters tend to keep the sweet, musical voices of their girlhood and that gives them a considerable and rather touching charm to which I am extremely sensitive. I find them at times superior to ourselves, and different for not having been obliged to face quite the same problems.

I wanted to say something to please her. 'When I was about seven years old', I said, 'my mother had sent me to a Catholic school attached to that other church in Clichy which had only just been built. Monseigneur Amette, Archbishop of Paris, later Cardinal, had been sent to consecrate it. Because I was blonde and rather pretty the headmistress chose me to present him with the illuminated address, but I was so nervous that I gave it to him upside-down.'

'Oh dear,' she exclaimed, 'how very interesting! Do you know what they did the other day to that church? Some of those people who have been desecrating things, writing insults on the tomb of the Unknown Soldier, and other acts of vandalism, threw a plastic bomb into it. The church is very badly damaged.'

'Yes, I read about that in the paper,' I said.

The porter at the town hall had posted himself like a watchdog within sight of my car, and I wanted to give him a small reward for his pains, but he utterly refused. I tried on my way back to the road to see something of the houses we lived in and the streets where I played, but I was tired and the traffic was dense.

Nevertheless I did discover the Rue Souchal where we lived for a time, and I even saw little girls on the pavement skipping and laughing as I used to do. How we used to race through the streets singing at the tops of our voices:

> Les pompiers de Nanterre
> Se sont fichus par terre
> Les pompiers de Clichy
> Sont des abrutis!

Which is all too childishly stupid to translate!

> The firemen of Nanterre
> Fell on their faces
> The firemen of Clichy
> Are just plain stupid!

# 8

M Y APARTMENT at the Plaza Athénée was full of red roses which my friend Georges Marin had sent me before leaving Paris for a week's holiday. My small car had brought me safely to my destination. The Champs Elysées glittered in the fierce sunshine, the heat forming a sort of mirage in the direction of the Étoile, but in the Avenue Montaigne the trees in full foliage gave shade, and it was with a feeling of thankfulness that I handed the car over to the porter, telling him to park it on the wide pavement and to leave it there in a safe place until I should need it again.

A bath was what I longed for and freedom in lighter clothes to walk without responsibility through the streets of the town. I would lose myself for a time as a spectator in a world—that of the XVIth *arrondissement*—eternally in contradiction with the one in which I had been brought up and yet tied mysteriously to it. Even as I went down in the lift, feeling lighter and refreshed, I was aware that, like the oft-quoted chameleon, my person was automatically adapting itself to its surroundings. My femininity, with its weaknesses and desires, bloomed to the contact of luxury, arrogantly impervious to the mean lodgings of my girlhood, the miserable insufficiencies of women like my mother's during her early married life, the present-day abomination of the Nanterre *bidonville*, in front of whose fountain of so little hope naked Arab and Portuguese children had come with a pitcher not three hours ago.

In the lift with me was an extremely pretty woman (I am much more generous in my appreciation of feminine beauty as I grow older) wearing a silk square. She was impeccably dressed and smelt good, but my sense of fashion told me that what I must take note of was the way her silk square, instead of being tied under her chin, was thrown slightly over one shoulder, which gave her a mocking, quizzical air which I found charming. Now I was all prepared for the passing pageant of the streets.

Passy stretches from the Place de l'Alma to the rural delights of the Bois de Boulogne. Its avenues are shining and wide, its vistas noble, its palaces, private houses and apartments luxurious with their walled gardens and tall, shady trees. The aggressiveness of its refinement and wealth is both modern and evocative of what one imagines of the magnificence and blinding beauty of Nineveh and Babylon. Few spots on our globe any longer dare to extol so openly with the blowing of golden trumpets what men and women can buy for themselves with money. Taxation and death duties have razed to the ground the mansions of a once privileged nobility in Park Lane and Berkeley Square, and a young and great queen drives democratically through a proud capital ennobled by a gradual distribution of its wealth. Thus there are occasions when London appears poor in comparison with certain aspects of Paris, the most anomalous of modern republics. In the XVIth *arrondissement* wealth positively shouts, deafens and blinds by its desire to remain for as long as possible in the hands of the few. Strong and mighty are the ramparts defending a mountain of gold that scarcely knew a tremor when the trees came crashing down in the Latin Quarter, when the Red and Black flags flew side by side above the Odéon. Now one prays (for what else can one pray for?) that the moment of danger is past. Now I can walk peacefully on this lovely afternoon along the wide Avenue du President Wilson, reflecting on the wisdom of Machiavelli who wrote: 'The one mistake that should never be made is to frighten, and not to strike!'

Here is the Place du Trocadero with its superb vista across the Seine to the Eiffel Tower, where two sets of memories superimpose themselves on my mind: the first when as a little girl I came to play here with my cousin Rolande, and dreamed of becoming one day a lady with a house in the XVIth *arrondissement*; the other when as a young married woman I came to the 1937 exhibition here and saw those two twin pillars, one surmounted by the swastika, the other by the hammer and sickle, that produced a panic within me that time will never efface.

The tourists on this June afternoon are few. Fear and a costly foreign exchange have made them rare. Some prefer to watch revolutions from a distance. The girls I meet are clearly native born, beautifully turned out, very assured of themselves, their split mini-skirts revealing a Bermuda of the same material as the outer garment so that with their slim legs and easy swinging step they look like Diana the huntress. I pass the establishment of a fashionable hairdresser whose display of human wigs in the window is as varied as the hats in the hatshops of my youth. The pavement smells good with an exotic mixture of famous perfumes escaping from the inside of the *salon*. What a feminine paradise! How I wish I had the time and the patience to submit myself to the vagaries of the great artist within. Youthful assistants, their hair beautifully styled, their impeccably white overalls ridiculously but charmingly short, look like shop window mannequins that might have suddenly come to life as in a ballet. Torn between the world of my youth and the world of my feminine desires, I feel rising up inside me an immense jealousy of those women who can afford to live in these apartment houses all about me, whose initial cost would scarcely be covered by a cheque for fifty thousand pounds. Add to this the running expenses, the maid, the rates, the *concierge*, the car and the daily ten-pound note in one's purse, and, in the end, I feel like a shepherdess in a seventeenth-century tale looking with longing at the prince in his castle. Alas, if I am ashamed of these feelings then what happens to romance!

I am on my way to visit my cousin Jean Le Bodo, who is one of France's great experts on rare books. His shop, a rendezvous for writers and bibliophiles, is in the Avenue Paul Doumer, but he lives with his wife Fernande in the Boulevard St Germain, in the heart of the Latin Quarter, so that I shall hear all about his grandstand view of the street fighting between the Sorbonne and the Odéon.

Here it is—the Livre de France. His own story is almost stranger than anything told in the rare and expensive tomes he sells.

Jean Le Bodo evoked for me the Touraine, the Loire and the strange figure of my maternal grandfather, the Zouave, who being poor sold himself twice into the army. The Zouave's sister, having left their birthplace Colmar when Alsace and Lorraine were annexed by the Germans after the war of 1870, followed the rabble of the army of the Loire, ending up at Tours, where she married a Breton and had two sons. This Breton, by name Le Bodo, had a barber's shop, and when Bernard, the elder boy, was still only five or six, he used to stand on a chair to shave his father's customers, saving the odd pennies he earned in tips to buy curious old books that he found in the boxes of second-hand dealers. He liked specially the ones with medieval pictures.

No French province was richer than the Touraine in old books, and little Bernard kept his treasures in a trunk, reading them over and over again. As nobody thought of sending him to school this was the only education he received, and soon the old way of writing French seemed as natural to him as the modern. On the death of his father Bernard, little more than a boy, took over the barber's shop and became head of the family, sending his young brother Louis to school for fear that by remaining at home too long with their mother he would talk with the guttural accent which had never left her because of an Alsatian upbringing.

Bernard was intelligent, but stunted and delicate. The two brothers worked side by side shaving the customers, but whenever Bernard could spare the time he would throw a sack over his shoulder and tramp through country lanes, calling at cottages, farms and châteaux for old books. Then he went farther to Vendôme, Blois, Loches and Chinon, coming back with church ornaments, illustrated missals and erotic books, all thrown together in the sack. His mother, old Mme Le Bodo, could not at all understand this method of trading, which consisted of buying and never selling. She used to wait for him to come back from his wanderings, and then ply him with such angry questions that he soon gave up trying to explain. He treated her with the utmost filial respect, but would say nothing, and she, finding herself thwarted, would complain to her younger son Louis, but Louis had faith in his brother, and would work twice as hard in the barber's shop every time that Bernard expressed a wish to go travelling.

At last Bernard's dream came true.

He opened a second-hand bookshop with volumes placed in trays outside. The barber's shop was sold, and Louis would

spend days alone in the bookshop while his brother went all over
the countryside. Sometimes Louis would stand in the doorway
looking at two pretty girls making hats in a modiste's shop on the
opposite side of the road. From time to time Jeanne, the younger
sister, would sling a bandbox under her arm and trip off to deliver
a hat. She noticed the young man smiling at her from his door-
step. She would smile back. They exchanged a few words, fell
in love and were married.

The two sisters went on making hats and the two brothers
continued to buy and sell books. Then Bernard fell in love with
Jeanne's elder sister Madeleine, and they too were married. The
Le Bodo brothers became so famous that Porto-Riche the playwright, Courteline the wit and Anatole France spent hours in
their shop. Their fame spread across France.

When I was sixteen I was taken by my Aunt Marguerite to stay
for a short time with Louis and his wife Jeanne at their house in
Tours. By then the two brothers had quarrelled. In appearance
Louis was still comfortably off, but unlike his brother, from
whom he had separated and who never ceased to gain importance,
Louis was on the verge of losing his fortune, though we knew
nothing of it. Each of the two now opposing houses had a son.
Bernard and Madeleine had Pierre, and Louis and Jeanne had
Jean. Once they had been brought up together. Now they were
kept apart, and when Madeleine and Jeanne, the two sisters, met
by accident in the street they pretended not to know each other.
The boy Jean was about eighteen when I arrived and was trying
to take his degree. I was rather dazzled by him.

The next time I went to Tours was just before my marriage.
When I called at Louis's once beautiful house the woman who
opened the door looked surprised. Louis Le Bodo had lost all
his money and the family had gone to Bordeaux in the hope of
buying and selling old books there, but shortly afterwards Louis
had died. His son Jean was married and had two sons. That was
all she could tell me.

Much later in Paris Fernande, Jean Le Bodo's wife, told me
about those days.

'The bookshop was tiny and there were five of us trying to
live on the proceeds. My mother-in-law generally looked after
it while Jean and his father would go to one of the châteaux of the
Loire to make a valuation. They sometimes stayed away for

several days. One day there was a ring at the door. It was very
hot and I was pregnant with my second boy. I dragged myself
down and was a good deal surprised to see Jean, whom I had
not expected till the following day.

'He put a finger to his lips to warn me not to speak and then
led me to a waiting cab, telling me to peep inside. Seated very
erect but as white as a piece of parchment was his father, who had
died suddenly while valuing some books in a château. Jean, with
the help of the cab-driver, had brought his father home, and now
left me alone with him while he went to break the news to his
mother in the shop.

'I was so overcome by the shock that I became covered with
red spots. We were at the end of our financial resources. This was
our worst time. Jean decided that as we could not be worse off
in Paris than we were in Bordeaux we would borrow the train
fare and leave. So we packed a crate of books and took third-class
tickets.'

I wish nobody a worse fate than to arrive penniless in Paris.
The Le Bodos with three boys starved for a time at the top of a
picturesque hovel built in 1590 and overlooking Notre Dame.
Such squalor and penury could no longer exist. Jean worked in a
second-hand bookshop in the Boulevard St Michel, Fernande
had one of those boxes for prints and books on the Quays. Their
climb back to fame and fortune was as much due to Fernande as
to Jean. She discovered, at what was then a very small rent, a
large apartment on the fifth floor of the unsmart end of the
Boulevard St Germain, the end with the shops and the chestnut
vendors and the girls who sell flowers under coloured umbrellas;
the noisy, crowded and picturesque end which leads into the
Boulevard St Michel, the end where all the rioting and burning
took place during the May 'revolution'.

Jean now made a place for me among the beautifully bound
sixteenth- and seventeenth-century treasures of the shop he now
owns in the most expensive part of Paris. He thus forms an intellectual bridge between the Latin Quarter and the homes and
palaces of the wealthy. His tasting of both white and black bread
have endowed him with gentle philosophy. Fernande was at
their country place at Roche-Posay. Their three sons, Christian,
Jacques and Michel, could hardly have been better placed to
witness recent events. Christian was one of the famous C.R.S.

special police in charge of motor-cycle units brought from all parts of France, Jacques was editor-in-chief of *Télé-7 Jours*, the equivalent of the B.B.C.'s *Radio Times* and Michel was a staff photographer on *Paris-Match*.

'The tear gas seeped through the closed doors and windows of the apartment and blinded us,' said Jean. 'Fernande went to our place in the country, and I remained alone most of the time. Fortunately I was able to move my car away quickly. Most of the others were overturned and burnt. I drove it through angry crowds as far as the Invalides where I thought it would be safer, and then came back in the early hours of the morning on foot. There was still heavy fighting round the Sorbonne, and the police, who had received instructions not to retaliate when paving stones were hurled at them, were exhausted. Three of them who saw me letting myself in at the street door told me that they had been on duty without food for fourteen hours, and did I know anywhere where they could buy a sandwich. There were no cafés open at that hour and all the shops had their iron shutters up. I led them up the five flights of stairs to the apartment and gave them a loaf of bread, some dried sausage, some cheese and a bottle of wine. I have seldom seen three such joyous policemen. As soon as they had finished they went back to go on being pelted with stones. My son Christian, meanwhile, who as you know was one of the motor-cycle escorts chosen to follow General de Gaulle, was assigned to special duties. Detachments of C.R.S. from Toulouse and Chateauroux were in camp just outside Paris to help their Paris colleagues. As they did not know their way about Christian used to convoy them in and out.

'I have no doubt from what my son told me and from what I saw myself that the special police needed considerable will-power and stamina to remain unflinching while they were being stoned and attacked with iron bars by professional agitators. As for the trees that were cut down in the Latin Quarter, it will take thirty years for new ones to grow to full height. I saw gangs of commandos arriving with high-speed saws to cut them down. Six of the largest trees were felled in as many minutes under my windows. That, you may be sure, was not the work of students.

'Now that it is over I retain strange pictures of those lurid nights and days, battles often waged under a cloud of government censorship. Much remains unexplained. There were acts of brutality, some photographed by my son Michel that can scarcely have been surpassed in the Spanish Civil War and that will never be revealed. There were small mysteries also such as the forty-odd youths and girls, clad in black shirts and red trousers or skirts, who marched past, led by commandos.'

For my cousin Jean Le Bodo, the 'revolution' of May was merely an interlude in his search for rare books and manuscripts, and soon he was telling me about a rare first edition of *Dominique* by Eugene Fromentin, owned by a man who lived in an old house near Chateauroux, but who for a long time refused to part with it. Then one day the owner said: 'If you want it so much, the novel must be unusually good. I will ask my wife to read it. She shall give me her opinion.' A month later Jean Le Bodo went to see him again: 'Well,' he asked, 'what did your wife say?'—'She thought it was terribly dull,' said the man. 'She didn't even finish it.'—'In that case', asked Jean, 'will you sell it to me?'—'Yes,' said the man, 'I will sell it to you, but just in case there's a catch in it I want twice as much as you offered me.' So Jean bought his first edition of Fromentin which has since been resold at a very high figure.

I told him that the books I would buy if I were rich were the eighteenth- and nineteenth-century children's books with those beautiful coloured plates. I wondered, for instance, how much a first edition of the *Malheurs de Sophie* would fetch.

'My son Jacques', he said, 'has two children. One Christmas I gave them some beautiful nineteenth-century children's books. I thought their father would be delighted. Instead he was angry. He said: "What do you mean by giving my children those books in which the hero was always being caned or made to stand in a corner wearing a dunce cap. Those books are full of brutality."'

Jean Le Bodo smiled.

'Alas,' he said, 'we don't cane our college boys any more. We are not even allowed to pull their ears or stand them in a corner. But were they so gentle at the Sorbonne last month?'

Taking leave of Jean Le Bodo, I walked slowly back towards the Avenue du Président Wilson. I found myself regretting the old Trocadero, vestige of the exhibition of 1878, not only because of the fun my cousin Rolande and I used to have playing against its walls, but because it was within its highly decorated interior that with the Protestant children of Clichy I was brought to pay homage in 1918 to President Woodrow Wilson himself who had come to lead the American delegation at the Versailles peace conference. With Simone and Mireille Maroger, the beautiful and gifted young daughters of our pastor, we had left Clichy very early that morning, passing through the fortifications and crossing Paris. All the children in that immense hall had been taught to sing the American national anthem, the Stars and Stripes flying proudly over our young heads. How proud and grateful we were to the Americans, with their young, clean-shaven faces and beautiful romantic uniforms for having come in their thousands across the Atlantic to save us! How we dreamed about their country, so vividly pictured in our minds through those early silent films! How excitedly we tasted the corned beef that came out of tins (to our immense surprise) and more or less prevented us from starving! Was it possible that within the short time between my girlhood and now there had grown up on television, radio and newspapers this insidious campaign of jealousy and hate against a nation which, by this time, had come not only once but twice to our rescue! If the 'revolution' of May had no other effect but to bring youth back to its senses in this respect, it would not have been unleashed in vain. As I thought about this a curious detail struck me. Whereas not so long ago insults against the Americans, tolerated by the administration, had been rife all over France, not a single one had I seen amongst all the writings on the walls at Nanterre! A subtle change was happening. It was as if, with fear in the air, we had suddenly been unshackled! The men who had fanned this hatred had been frightened for their own skins. They were less arrogant, less proud!

As children we were taught that the Trocadero stood on high ground where in the seventh century a village dominated the Seine. Charles I of England's queen, Henrietta Maria, founded a convent here, and this takes me back to my own girlhood when, during visits to my cousin Rolande, I had an inexplicable admiration for the English nannies who used to congregate with their prams in this part of the XVIth *arrondissement* where their charges could play in peace and safety. My desire to become bilingual must have dated from this time, which tends to show to what extent the little girl is the future woman.

While attending the Versailles peace conference President Woodrow Wilson stayed with Francis de Croisset, the famous playwright, in one of the loveliest houses hereabouts, in what was aptly called Place des États Unis. This superb residence had belonged to Mme de Croisset's first husband, father of the celebrated Marie-Laure de Noailles who just about this time was a beautiful young girl. During a visit to Oxford with her mother she was to spend enchanting hours with my future husband, then an undergraduate at Magdalen, drifting in a punt down the Cherwell, heavy with the scent of May trees. By the time I was married, Marie-Laure, having come of age, had inherited the house, while Francis de Croisset, his wife and their son Philippe were living in an apartment at the smart end of the Boulevard St Germain.

I was of course invited, and this was my first contact with the literary world of Paris. The playwright's study was a very large room whose french windows opened on to a terrace that led into a garden, in the middle of which was a beautiful old tree. The walls of the room were entirely covered from floor to ceiling with bookcases containing leather-bound volumes and yellow paperbacks. I had never before seen so many books in the possession of a single man and, because I was still very young and naïve, I was enthralled by the small stair ladder on wheels, with its polished wood hand-rail, used for reaching volumes on the higher shelves. On an easel stood the portrait in oils of the writer's son, tall, blond, aristocratic, descending on his mother's side from the Chevignés and the Marquis de Sade—Philippe de Croisset. The moment came when a footman in livery and white gloves slid open some doors and announced that the meal was served. This was the end of my peace of mind. We sat down at a dazzlingly set table with silver and wine glasses shining on the beautiful white linen cloth. As I was the only woman among a distinguished company of men, to me fell the honour of being served first. I would not have felt more embarrassed if I had been offered the trophy of the hunt by the Sun King, Louis XIV, in person. Gloved hands were holding in front of me a silver dish on which was an immense fish half wrapped in a napkin.

What on earth was I to do? My panic must have been visible. My eyes must have sent distress signals to my host who in the sweetest possible way, as if I had been a little girl, broke into the agony of my uncertainty to serve me himself, never ceasing the while to continue an erudite conversation with the table as a whole. This, I think, besides the admiration I had for him as a writer (he was the darling of the Boulevard theatres), made me sense that there was something specially nice about him, and as the meal progressed I became a great deal less nervous. But what an education in the habits of another world still lay before me.

'It must be lovely to live in the very heart of Paris and to have such a beautiful garden all to yourself,' I said to him as we went back into his study. It was one of those hot nights when Paris was particularly stifling.

'Yes,' said Francis, 'Mme de Croisset who has gone to the theatre this evening with friends has a great affection for that old tree, and often on warm nights she has a camp bed made up on the lawn, and in the morning I find her asleep under the boughs of the tree.'

The fads of the wealthy struck me as passing strange, sleeping out in the open, under the trees, like a tramp!

Francis de Croisset was to remain till the end of his life one of our closest friends. We had merely to ask him: 'We would like to meet this person or that,' and immediately the matter was arranged. Gone is his world of the glittering boulevards, of Robert de Flers, of Lucien and Sacha Guitry, of Maurice Donnay and Jean Richepin, of Jean Forain, one of the world's greatest caricaturists, and of Francisque Poulbot, who immortalized the children of the Paris streets, especially of the days of my youth in Montmartre. Fortune had smiled on Francis de Croisset from an early age. I once heard Maurice Sachs tell how Sarah Bernhardt liked to appear at receptions with one hand dramatically on the shoulder of the budding young dramatist who at twenty had already made a name for himself by collaborating with Maurice Leblanc in a stage adaptation of *Arsène Lupin*. There were times when no fewer than three theatres of the Paris boulevards were running different plays by Francis de Croisset, while at the same time a novel or a travel book under his signature would be in the windows of the book shops. His admiration for the English stage (he loved thrillers and ghost stories) was always bringing him to London where he would cut as smiling, though as modest, a figure in London literary circles as at some official reception at Buckingham Palace. It was part of his character that he had friends in all worlds, and knew how to charm such military giants of his day as Joffre or Lyautey, as easily as wits like Clément Vautel who wrote an enchanting column every morning on the front page of the old *Journal*. He was of course utterly bilingual, and the sad, disillusioned 28th President of the United States and he became fast friends. Thus when I pass along the Avenue du Président Wilson I like to think that it was this president who on 2nd April 1917 asked Congress to declare war on Germany and come to the help, among others, of a nation who just now seemed temporarily to forget it. I also like to think of the man of so many parts who played host to him, and who now lay buried at the far end of the tiny Passy cemetery which is almost opposite the Trocadero.

This was not the first time I had turned into this curiously shadeless retreat. As a girl I had been taken there by my Aunt Marie-Thérèse who had a mania for historical novels and cemeteries. She said they helped her to understand history, and that if one approached tombstones in the right way they were not at all depressing. She and my mother were brought up by my grandmother, the wife of the Zouave, at Blois. Here the two little girls had enough history to fill their inquiring minds.

While my grandmother, who was something of a witch, went off to wash linen in the Loire and dream her fantastic dreams, Marie-Thérèse and Matilda were left to look after themselves. Marie-Thérèse, the elder sister, would take the younger sister Matilda, whom she adored, by the hand into the château where she would teach her to read on the medieval tombstones. By making her spell out not only the lettering but also the dates, she gave her an excellent grounding in spelling, arithmetic and history all at one go, which stood Matilda later in very good stead. For my mother, who had practically no schooling in the modern sense of the word, wrote excellent concise prose, had great observation and I never knew her to make a mistake either in English or in French.

In the tiny Passy cemetery, on a grey stone near the far wall,
this inscription is to be found:

Comte Adheaume de Chevigné
1847–1911
Miss Frances Smiley
dec 6 Jul 1931
Comtesse de Chevigné
1859–1938
Francis de Croisset
1876–1937
Gustave Daudin
notre serviteur
1876–1940
Mme Francis de Croisset
1880–1963
Philippe de Croisset
1911–1965

Here, in a few lines, was the story of a family.

First there was the count, the aristocrat, descendant of a great
and proud lineage, whom I never knew, followed long afterwards
by the obscure English governess who, as in a novel by the
Brontës, had devoted her entire life to the family, identifying
herself with it to such an extent that nobody knew even the date
or the circumstance of her birth in England. Then came the
Comtesse de Chevigné, feared for her caustic tongue, of which
many stories were told. This descendant of the Marquis de Sade,
whom my husband as an Oxford undergraduate met in the Place
des Etats Unis, was a formidable figure of a kind now totally
forgotten. Francis de Croisset, that brilliant youth of twenty who
was to add his own literary achievements to a family already
celebrated for its eminence in diplomacy, high finance and
letters. Philippe, the good-looking young man whose portrait
on an easel in his father's book-lined study had intrigued me, was
brought here before his time, killed instantly when his car hit a
tree while he was driving to the South of France to attend to an
estate his mother had left at the time of her death two years
earlier. He was thought to have fallen asleep at the wheel.

Before we turn away from this family story, consider also the case of Gustave Daudin, already mentioned, who at his death earned this simple title: *notre serviteur*. I find something biblical in the noble simplicity of these two words, as if perhaps we are apt to misjudge the nobility of servitude.

How I sympathize with my aunt's fascination with these evocations of the past. I am sorry for the misguided men who during the May 'revolution' daubed war memorials with paint. I would have brought them in front of the grave of this young man, Chevalier de la Légion d'honneur, Croix de Guerre, who volunteered at the age of seventeen and was killed in aerial combat on 7th September 1918 at the age of twenty.

Ah, this great piece of polished black marble has nothing but the name on it! Is the name so famous that it requires no date, no description, no other passport into heaven?

### Pearl White

She made me scream in admiration when I was a little girl during the First World War. Her blonde beauty, like that of Mary Pickford, was unforgettable. Tied by villains to the railroad track, she struggled in vain to free herself while one of those huge American locomotives with clanging bell came rushing towards her. Every Saturday night Matilda and I set off through the darkened streets of war-time Clichy to the local cinema to watch the latest episode in the adventures of Pauline, alias Pearl White. How she made us love the great American scene. How we turned to her in our desperate need to forget the horrors of Verdun. I even recall in detail how she was dressed—a skin-tight black tailor-made, out of whose long tight sleeves fell waves of frilly white lace. Oh, how I dreamed about her! All too often, for I was still very young, I fell asleep before the end of the episode. During the whole of the ensuing week I would ply Matilda with questions: 'How did it end? How did Pauline escape?'

These were the things that made us love America. The silent films, opening up in our minds a vast, wonderful new way of life, and then the arrival of those magnificent, smiling, clean-shaven young men who appeared to us like knights in armour come to save us from oblivion. How could we not have loved this distant land of freedom and opportunity?

From the street this small cemetery of Passy is dominated by a mausoleum surmounted by the cross of the Russian Orthodox

Church. Indeed the casual passer-by might think that the cemetery was entirely devoted to persons of that faith, whereas this ornate memorial is the only one of its kind, and devoted to a girl of twenty-four, whose enthusiasms and ambitions filled her with a desire for immortal fame. Let us approach and read some of the writing inscribed on the four sides.

'Oh, Marie! Oh, white lily! Radiant beauty! Her name is immortal and burns like a torch!'

There are parallel lists of her books and of her paintings, and the date of her birth at Poltava, in Russia—1860.

What is immortality? Has Marie Bashkirtseff attained it? One supposes that she has, for the diary in which she began to record her joys and sorrows at the age of thirteen, and which she continued to the time of her death, is one of those human, intensely feminine documents that time will never wither. For me there is the added poignancy that she went to Pau, as I did as a girl, to try to cure the illness that finally overcame her.

I was so exhausted by this long walk that, on leaving the cemetery, I hailed a passing cab. The cab was quite luxurious, and its owner-driver, who had been listening to a political commentary on the second part of the general elections which were to take place the following day, asked me with unaccustomed politeness whether he should turn it off. I signified my indifference. Even if it had vexed me I would not have dared object.

A moment later, however, he switched the radio off of his own accord and decided to talk.

'They'll win of course', he said, 'with a huge majority. That's obvious.'

'I suppose it is.'

'As far as we owner-drivers are concerned things can hardly get any worse. We went on strike like everybody else. What else could we do? There was no point in taking the risk of having our cabs overturned and set on fire, and no insurance to cover us against that sort of thing. Business is bad enough as it is without that! The summer so far has been a positive disaster.'

'Even before the rioting?'

'Even before the rioting. Not an American tourist! Nobody from Britain! Hardly a tourist at all in fact. They stay home or cut

Paris out of their itinerary. It's not to be wondered at, is it? I
don't say that the General is wrong all the time, but the way he
sent the Americans packing as if they had stolen the family
silver! That's not the way to treat a nation who came to our help
in two world wars! The only visitors who seem to think they are
welcome are the Arabs and the Negroes. Instead of all the money
we spend on the bomb and the undeveloped countries we would
do better to look after our own people. Prestige! What's prestige
abroad? Does that fill our bellies?'

'You have been given permission to put your fares up, I see.'

'Yes, and about time too. Not only is there no tourist traffic,
but most of the streets or avenues in the centre of the city have
become bottlenecks. One can't even guarantee getting a person
to a main line railway station in time to catch a train. Well, here's
the Avenue Montaigne. What do you do at the Plaza Athénée?
You live there?'

I let pass the impertinence of his query and answered:
'Occasionally, but I left my small house in Normandy very
early this morning.'

'Ah!' he said, pleased to have discovered that much about me.
'My wife's family comes from there.'

I telephoned friends and changed to feel cool at dinner. Since
the Avenue Montaigne had become a one-way street the noise
even fairly high up had become deafening, and I wondered what
people thought about it who had paid a king's ransom for pent-
houses here not so long ago, when the thick foliage of the trees
sufficed to deaden the roar of the traffic. But now there was not
only the noise, but the ceaseless smell of fuel oil. Could it be that
I was already missing the pure air of our orchards? I hoped we
would find somewhere quiet to dine in the open air. There was a
pleasant restaurant near the gardens of the Luxembourg. We
could stroll along the Boulevard St Michel and have a look at the
Sorbonne to see if there were any battle scars.

I put on Ferragamo shoes which would be both elegant and
comfortable and went down to wait in the hall.

We hailed a taxi and told him to drive us to the corner of the
Boulevard St Germain and the Boulevard St Michel. He could
drop us off at the Musée Cluny and from there we would stroll

for half an hour through the Latin Quarter, deciding on the spur of the moment where we would dine. The traffic was appalling, but at last we came in sight of the Marché St Germain where my cousin Jean le Bodo was dispatched by Fernande every Sunday morning to buy the week's ration of cheese. In Fernande's family a meal that does not end with cheese is just not to be contemplated. 'But', she once confessed to me, 'the choosing of cheese is a man's job. Only a man has the courage, the audacity, to open a box of Camembert in full sight of the vendor, smell it knowingly and press the paper with his thumb to test its degree of ripeness. Or to point to the piece of Roquefort that he believes exactly right for his particular taste. Any housewife who tried that sort of thing would be told to keep her hands off the merchandise, you can be sure of that. What with a shopping basket, a purse and the other encumbrances that we women trail around with us when we go shopping, we would end by having to accept what we were offered. At one time when I was less artful I did do my best to buy the week's cheese, but as soon as I put it on the table my husband or one of the boys would be certain to exclaim: "My poor Fernande, who let you in for this terrible cheese?" So I hit on a plan. I flattered my husband, telling him that women really knew nothing about cheese. Would he not come to our rescue and go every Sunday morning to market at St Germain and choose it himself? My husband preened himself and agreed. As a result I was left in peace every Sunday to get on with the lunch. Since then we have never had an argument about the cheese. If the Camembert is dry, or too hard or too soft, if the Roquefort is too strong or too salt, the fault is due to the weather, the moon or to politics. It is never my husband's fault. A man's judgment, when it comes to choosing cheese, is infallible!'

When, in addition to her husband, she had three sons at home, the C.R.S., the journalist and the photographer, Fernande once said to me: 'You have no idea what it means to have four men's shirts to wash and iron twice a week—and one of them a police-man's shirt, the shirt of a special policeman who is practically the head of state's personal, trick cyclist bodyguard! Oh, the starching and the ironing.'

We had just risen from a meal and Fernande, taking off the precious flowered oilcloth which never needed washing, only a damp cloth passed over it, carefully rolled it over a broom handle so that the varnish would not crack when it was stored away. I hated the irksomeness but admired her parsimony. When we last met she, who by her energy and faith had led the family out of misery, exclaimed: 'We are well off now. We have virtually more money than we need. But half the time money comes too late!'

We paid off the taxi and walked towards the Sorbonne. In front of the buildings were a considerable number of police with their cars ranged alongside.

Which of the student leaders are we to believe when it comes to analysing the beginnings of this strange but frightening revolution? In the days of the French Impressionists there was a café concert song that started: 'A nation is strong when it knows how to read.' We are told that some at least of the trouble started because the sons and daughters of the so-called working classes were getting less favoured treatment at the universities than those of the professional or executive classes. This was not quite true, but even so the subject was already much in the wind in Eugène Manuel's day. 'Who was Eugène Manuel?' you ask. A gentle poet who more or less spanned Queen Victoria's reign and who wrote a play called *Les Ouvriers—The Workmen*, produced at the Comédie-Française. Its hero proclaimed:

> I learn to draw at home, I visit the museums,
> I follow public lectures and classes,
> I learn more or less to reason intelligently.

and so on, until at last by the time the curtain falls, he has achieved happiness through culture, as in all good Communist countries, and even as in Hitler's Germany.

Other student leaders tell us that there never was any snobbery at the Sorbonne, and that the will to acquire learning has never been impeded in France. Was Diderot not the son of a humble cutler at Langres? (I remember being given as a little girl a dictation in *Chosen Pieces*, describing how Diderot's father wept with joy at the sight of his son returning to school with his satchel.) They claimed that student unrest sprang from something quite different, from a deep-rooted conviction that every faculty should prepare its students for safe jobs awaiting them in industry, science or the arts. The budding industrialist must be sure of becoming a future Marcel Boussac, the scientist a Marcel Das-

seault, the art student a Sartre or a Picasso. In short that the
university must be a passport to a sure job, a big salary and, if
possible, a private aeroplane.

Even the President of the Republic was quoted as saying that
every university course should correspond exactly with something for which there was direct need in public life. Pierre
Gaxotte, the greatest of contemporary historians, a member of
the French Academy, took the opposite view. He claimed that
this was not the function of a university. Nobody would contest
the excellence of creating, in close collaboration with industry,
agriculture and commerce, new technical institutes to feed them.
That was fine. But a Faculty of Letters, such as the Sorbonne,
should form the mind, teaching a superior form of culture, *not*
specially adapted to any particular trade or profession. To try to
make of the higher rungs of intellectual education, nothing but
the guaranteed promise of a place or of a job, was to degrade it
entirely. The professors themselves would become nothing more
than members of an employment agency.

For the moment everybody, both parents and students, not to
mention the public, was in such a dither that nobody even lifted
an eyebrow when he read on some grey, dark wall:

> No more baccalauréat!
> No more eliminations!
> No more finals!
> No more professors over forty!
> Down with everybody in authority!
> Death to the police!

Parents, who had started off by sympathizing with their
children, now gave up trying to understand altogether, and
thought it high time to give them a spanking and put them to
bed. Even the actors and actresses of both the state and boulevard
theatres who had all hailed the students of Nanterre and the
Sorbonne when the trouble began, helping to run up the Red
Flag, and closing their own theatres so that they could go on
strike, were slowly waking up, rubbing their eyes, after this
midsummer night's dream. A suggestion had even been made
that in a truly democratic world the stage should not be reserved
for purely professional actors and actresses, but that any person
so inclined should have the right to walk on and declaim the lines

of Molière and Shakespeare. 'But already half the progressive professional actors and actresses in Paris are out of work!' objected a voice in an early 'dialogue'.

We passed a quiet hotel, the sort one expects to see in the Latin Quarter, facing the Sorbonne. It had this notice pinned to the door: *Nous demandons 1 femme de chambre*—'We want 1 chambermaid'. What, I wondered, had happened to the former chambermaid? Had she fled in panic because of the noise, the broken windows, the tear gas bombs, the stabbing. I would have liked to go in and apply for the job. It would have been fun to write the journal of a chambermaid facing the Sorbonne. We crossed the Boulevard St Michel where I counted more than eight trees cut down in a row—trees in the full vigour of their growth and summer beauty. What a noble victory for poets to sing!

The Médicis Brasserie, overlooking the Gardens of the Luxembourg, was closed. We had vaguely thought of dining there. We would find plenty of other places. Soon we were at the back of the Odéon, that annexe of the Comédie-Française that had played such a major and shameful role in the 'revolution' of May. Originally built by Poupart-Dorfeuille in 1797, it was twice burnt, and finally rebuilt with its stately columns and steps in 1819 when Napoleon was dying at St Helena. In 1946 it was annexed to the Comédie-Française for the production of more modern plays.

The Red Flag was already down, and the Tricolour, proud but limp because there was no breath of wind, had taken its place. Occupied on 15th May, the theatre became the symbol of the students' cultural revolution against what they termed the bourgeois, middle-class theatre. Under the slogan 'Imagination takes Power', the hall was turned, at first with some actor co-operation, into a non-stop debating society which soon ran dry of subjects to invent. The theatre then degenerated into a place of indescribable filth, in part a hide-out for the so-called armed Katangese, and in part a brothel and a refuge for the rabble.

On 14th June Paris police belatedly emptied the theatre and arrested the fugitive mercenaries and their pitiful hangers-on.

We were passing along the side of the theatre on our way to the square in front of it. Here we saw the thing that more than all the rest, more than every absurdity and horror of the last two months, made me sick with the abomination and shame. To hide what I felt would be to remove from these events what was low and cowardly, to allow others to believe that every explosion of youth must of necessity be fine and noble because it springs in the first place from youth—a movement for future generations to emulate.

Right along the wall in immense letters of fire, I read this horrible prayer:

*De Gaulle! Mon Dieu, faites qu'il crève!*

For that I absolved him of all the faults his puny enemies had the temerity to accuse him. He was greater than any of them. I saw him a man to be honoured for his suffering. If, on the next day, I had been called upon to vote, I would have voted for him like all the rest of the nation.

In the square, which was almost deserted on this lovely hot summer evening, opposite the pillars of the theatre, there is a famous restaurant where I had several times dined with friends in the past. Hydrangeas and little red lamps decorated the white tables on the terrace. I think that normally I would have sat down gratefully at one of these delightful tables and allowed myself to be ordered a quiet supper. But, in truth, the writing on the wall had turned my stomach and I had no desire to eat in front of this revolting sacrilege. I had no doubt that the giant would soon in some powerful roar of his majestic voice shatter the ranks of these ill-mannered students, these 'little darlings' who wrote low insults on theatre walls. I wanted to get back into the Boulevard St Michel. Here there were the usual cafés with their summer crowds, but things had changed a lot since the days of Hemingway. Things were harder, more cruel.

'I don't want to dine on the Left Bank at all!' I suddenly exclaimed. 'Let us go somewhere entirely different, to the Place des Vosges, for instance.'

The Place des Vosges, begun under Henry IV of France, and finished under Louis XIII, the monarch of the *Three Musketeers*, with its arcades and beautiful gardens, is one of the architectural jewels of Europe. At one of the corners, unchanged since he lived there, is Victor Hugo's house in which he wrote *Hernani*, the play which produced a battle between classics and romantics on its first night in February 1830.

The first time I saw this superb square was during the First

World War. My cousin Ernestine, a beautiful girl of twenty, with whom every man fell in love, had come to Paris from the Midi because her young husband Toulouse was wounded, and my mother had invited her to stay with us. She told us one morning that she was anxious to visit some Toulouse cousins who lived in this quiet square, and so my mother allowed me to go with her. Secretly, I think, my mother hoped that Ernestine would want to spend the rest of her stay in Paris with them. They were richer than we were, and therefore in a better position to lodge her.

Though I was only ten, the Place des Vosges made such an impression on me that I never forgot it. Perhaps it was for this reason, shaken by what I had seen on the Left Bank, that I wanted to rediscover my girlhood. Though events in France at that time had been so utterly miserable, children often lived screened from the harsh realities in a world of their own. And my world at that time was often full of delight.

I recall wide dark stairs, a bell which Ernestine rang and a high-ceilinged room in which stood a young soldier, the son of the house, who was on leave from the trenches. The young man was collarless and in his shirt sleeves. His sky blue army trousers were held up by braces which reminded me, for some reason, of a horse's harness. His prominent Adam's apple and his braces combined to shock the naïve little girl that I then was, but Ernestine obviously thought him very handsome.

The young man took great pains to make himself agreeable to Ernestine, and he took us into a kitchen with tall windows through which one could see all the glory of the square. The Toulouse cousin whom Ernestine had come to visit was at the kitchen table peeling such an enormous pile of potatoes that I wondered how she would ever get to the end of them. I was reminded of those impossible tasks that witches in fairy books set to their heroines.

Ernestine began to talk about Toulouse and how nobly he had fought and had been wounded. She called him 'my Henry', and while she prattled away in her hot Midi accent the young soldier, still in his braces, took a chair and sat beside her, gradually edging closer and closer.

Standing over by the window, I thought about lunch and how on earth we would ever find our way back to Clichy.

As the morning wore on, the mountain of potatoes became a

sizzling pan of french fried, and these, with a bottle of red wine from the Midi, were placed on a white cloth on the kitchen table. How delicious it all was!

After lunch we were escorted back to the nearest underground station by the soldier, now in his tunic, and with his arm round Ernestine's waist in order, so he said, to protect this poor little provincial girl from the dangers of the Paris streets. But Ernestine threw her head back and laughed her warm, sensual laugh. When we finally arrived back at Clichy it was not Ernestine but I who received a scolding from my mother, who had imagined me run over or raped.

Now on this June evening, so many years later, I rediscovered all the beauty of the magnificent setting. We had been driven there by a taxi-driver who told us that he had spent all the evening driving Parisians and their children to the various main line railway stations for the start of their summer holidays. We paid him off outside one of those famous restaurants whose little red lamps make splashes of colour under the arcades. It was warm enough to sit out in a dress or a blouse, though occasionally a slight wind blew from the direction of Victor Hugo's house!

The table next to ours was occupied by a young couple, the girl elegant, the man, already important, sure of himself, very attentive, helping her to compose a menu she would enjoy, ordering an excellent champagne without fuss. When the *maître d'hôtel* had gone I ceased to be interested, but much later, during a pause in our own conversation, we caught these words that struck us curiously.

'Yes,' the man said, 'but that was before the revolution.'

I was myself hungry but still not tired. I had hoped not to be disappointed in this restaurant. It seemed important to me that nothing should mar the happiness of my memories. Well, what we were served was in line with the highest French cuisine, and the fried potatoes, made freshly for us, were just as good as those I had eaten with Ernestine.

Afterwards we walked a little way under the arcades where there were a few shops, nearly all expensive antique furniture shops, arranged amusingly to give the effect of a seventeenth- or eighteenth-century room with everything that would normally have been in it, like a reconstruction in the Victoria and Albert

Museum in South Kensington. We went through the gardens to admire the statue of Louis XIII and then out into the crowded, busy, populous rue St Antoine, where the Grande Mademoiselle during the Fronde gave orders for the cannon to be fired at the musketeers of Louis XIII. Along this wide, noisy road, with its cobblestones, rolled the carts carrying victims to the guillotine during the French Revolution.

Thus looking at the shop windows, talking, mingling with the crowds, enjoying the midnight air we reached the Paris Halles, equivalent of our Covent Garden market, and doomed like Covent Garden to disappear from the heart of the city. Here lorries bringing fruit and vegetables from the South of France were already being unloaded on the pavement.

Soon we reached that immense store, the Bazaar de l'Hôtel de Ville, where a great display was being made of garden mowers in one of the windows. This is indeed for the French a great change in the pattern of suburban life, or even in country life, now that everybody owns a secondary residence. Gone are the vegetable patches of my girlhood. The leeks, onions and potatoes that went into the nightly tureen of soup, once that sign of a comfortable home and family happiness, are no longer lovingly and tenderly grown in a kitchen garden. Everything is far too much trouble to produce out of the soil. What are the super-markets for? Or those canned goods from distant countries with trade agreements? A neatly kept lawn has become a status symbol —and a lawnmower, petrol-driven of course, can be purchased so easily, like the washing-machine and the refrigerator, on delightful credit, with not even a centime down!

The great fruit and vegetable market groaned and stretched its limbs like an awakening giant, injecting nocturnal activity into a dozen small, mysteriously lit streets on our right, while to the left of us all the history of a nation, the Hôtel de Ville, the Tour St Jacques, the Sainte Chapelle, the Louvre, cast their silhouettes against the dark, fast-flowing waters of the Seine. The cafés, famous for onion soup served to market porters, poets and men of letters in the small hours, were furbishing zinc counters and marble-topped tables. A provocatively dressed young woman slunk past slate-grey walls and stood immobile in front of the lighted sign of a cheap hotel.

I have never had the slightest desire to be a man. On the contrary I rejoice in the good fortune that made me a woman, but I envy in them their ability to wander unnoticed through colourful, exciting, ill-famed streets, or along the waterfront of foreign ports, or in markets in the small hours of the morning, listening, observing, exchanging conversation in bars with strangers, taking in the sort of atmosphere that can only be mine in imagination.

I would have been quite willing to walk back to the Avenue Montaigne if I had not suddenly become so tired, but in front of the Louvre I cried mercy, and as there was no taxi in sight we delved down into the métro.

The Paris underground has become nearly as expensive as a taxi in the old days. The booking clerk was knitting a baby's vest, with busy fingers soiled by what Émile Zola called the dirt of money. One was sorry to disturb her, but mechanically she laid the piece of knitting down and handed one ticket and change.

Two German *au pair* girls were sitting on the platform bench, waiting for a train and exchanging confidences. Our train arrived almost silently, and three stations later we left it to emerge half way up the Champs Elysées. The famous thoroughfare was crowded and extremely gay even at this hour. Catching sight of a chemist's shop I suddenly remembered that I wanted a different-coloured nail varnish to wear at tomorrow's wedding. I should have written at 'today's' wedding, for it was long past midnight. It was to attend this wedding that I had primarily come to Paris. Today was Danièle Pradeau's great day. How excitedly she must at this moment have been thinking of her wedding dress and all the last minute preparations for the ceremony.

This chemist's shop in the Champs Élysées was of rather a special kind, shaped like a railway coach with a narrow corridor separating show cases which were full of every kind of make-up and beauty preparation. Behind the long counter trained assistants were constantly checking goods and invoices. There was never any question of a shade of lipstick, eye shadow or nail varnish being out of stock. One merely chose from a coloured card and mentioned the corresponding number.

I studied the Christian Dior card and chose Number 74! An assistant I had seen here many times before (she has all her pharmaceutical degrees) emerged from behind the counter. When she had discovered the small package we opened it, our heads close together, our expressions registering great seriousness, to make sure that neither of us had made a mistake and that it was indeed the colour I had chosen.

So out once again into this miraculous sweet night to resume our wanderings. Thanks to my Ferragamo shoes and the fact that the heels were not too pointed or too high, we descended the rue Pierre-Charron, along the Avenue Montaigne, to a restaurant called the Bar of the Artists, because at varying times of the day or night it becomes the rendezvous of model girls from Christian Dior or Madeleine de Rauch, of the girls who work at the great hairdressing establishments such as that of the Carita Sisters, or of actors and actresses before or after performances, at theatres like the Théâtre des Champs Élysées.

The barmen wore red jackets and the beer was excellent. Somewhere on the opposite side of the avenue the windows of my apartment were open on the night. Bed was waiting for me, but during the effervescence of this hour between night and morning I began to think about my hens in their hen-house, about the five little chicks I had bought at Dozulé market and who never went to perch with the big one until I had given them their bread and milk. How puzzled they must have been not to see me this evening! I had brought ten back from Dozulé in a cardboard box with holes punched at the sides; because of the abominable weather I lost half of them in spite of the fact that I had tended them, when they had been ill, as a real English nanny would have tended her charges. I brought them into the kitchen and allowed them to sleep near the warmth of the Aga. What were the cats doing? Were they all three asleep in the basket I had prepared for them?

Well, in a few hours I would begin another day!

I rang very early for breakfast.

Country habits are not easily changed, and at home this was the hour of the day I liked best when, while allowing the boiling water to seep through the coffee percolator, I opened the hen-houses, scattered the grain, prepared bread and milk for the chickens, the cats and the birds, and then went to inspect the roses in the garden.

Breakfast is delightful also in Paris, but for different reasons. The coffee is less hot, is never quite as I make it myself, but the china is lighter and more pleasing to the eye and the touch. I have more time to devote to my appearance. The nail varnish I bought in the Champs Elysées was even prettier by daylight than I had expected. Why did I not buy two bottles instead of only one? Why was I always so terrified to overspend? I would try to go back to the same shop. I must also find time to go to Guerlain, even though this meant crossing the Champs Elysées and walking quite a distance. To go to the House of Guerlain, even for the slightest purchase, a pot of cream, for instance, was in itself exciting, like going to a great dressmaker to buy a dress, or to Carita Sisters to have one's hair styled differently. These were things that gave me a wonderful feeling of contentment.

The sun was streaming through the wide open windows of my bedroom, and the maid had deposited the *Figaro*, the *New York Herald-Tribune* and a London newspaper on my table. I did so wish I had a pretty print dress to wear at the wedding. I would bake in a skirt and a silk blouse. Fortunately I did not need to worry about a hat. One hardly ever saw a woman wearing a hat any longer in Paris, though I must confess that there was a modiste in the Avenue Paul Doumer in which I saw some very pretty ones and felt a sudden desire to go in.

I started telephoning friends—Mme Renée de Monbrison, for instance, whose beautiful antique furniture shop in the rue Jacob in the Latin Quarter was in the front line of fire. I thought I would have time to dash round and see her but she was on the point of leaving Paris. She said that her mother, who was ninety-four, was as perky as a girl and just now was staying with her sister Yvonne at Wing, near Leighton Buzzard. Another friend was at her house in Thuir near Perpignan. I would dawdle all the morning, lunch in the Bois and arrive at the church just in time for the ceremony.

Neuilly in early afternoon was like an oven, with the sun beating down on streets and avenues jammed with parked or crawling cars. The church of St John the Baptist was separated from the avenue by a narrow street running parallel to it, but which, like all the others, had cars parked fender to fender all along it. Philippe Pradeau was welcoming friends at the top of the steps. Inside the church Dr Salmont and his American-born wife, Danièle's grandparents, were standing by the altar rail and I went to embrace them. Both were nervous and much affected, for this was the first of their grandchildren to be married. Andrée, Danièle's mother, was wearing a wide-brimmed hat of navy blue straw.

Now the church began to fill up and the bride, in her long white wedding dress and veil, arrived up the aisle on her father's arm. In his address Abbé Ouvrard, chaplain of Notre Dame, recalled the tragedy of Andrée's brother Bernard who went back to rejoin the Resistance movement after going to the nursing home to see his sister who had just given birth to Danièle, and less than a week later, on 10th August 1944, was assassinated by the Germans.

Suddenly from a side aisle of this church, the nave of which by now was full of guests, came the vigorous yelling of a baby being brought by his parents for christening in a Lady Chapel. A priest led this small procession, and the baby's young godmother, wearing a fashionable mini-skirt, held the infant preciously in her arms, the baby's long robes contrasting with the shortness of the girl's skirt. The baby continued to yell which, according to the old wives' tales of my youth, was a sign that it would be attended by good fortune throughout its life. Even before the Abbé Ouvrard had finished his address the christening was finished and the procession returned whence it came. Soon the organ played the Wedding March, the guests rose and we became aware, looking about us, that all our friends from the village had come to witness Danièle's happiness. Annette Laurent, elegant in an emerald silk tailor-made, interrupted a conversation with her friend Mme Dumesnil to greet me, asking: 'Are you going back to the country tonight?'—'I think so.'—'Oh, darling, *do* let me have some of those delicious eggs from your farm tomorrow morning. All the family will be there.'

Meanwhile Andrée Pradeau's farmers, the husband, the wife and all the children, were there, looking sunburnt, rosy-cheeked and very shy and important in their Sunday best clothes. They had driven to Paris after milking the cows that same morning, and had arrived in their small car only just in time, stopping triumphantly at the bottom of the church steps where Philippe Pradeau, in his morning coat with the white carnation in it, was receiving his guests.

'My goodness,' said Philippe Pradeau to M. Dénos his farmer, 'just look at your car!'

The farmer looked puzzled. 'What's the matter with it?' he asked. 'We did the journey with all the family on board in just over four hours.'

'Yes,' said Philippe Pradeau, laughing, 'but you chose this very moment to burst a tyre!'

The reception in the grounds of the Tir aux Pigeons in the Bois de Boulogne brought us all together again in a countrified setting. I ate the first peach of the summer and drank to the bride's health in a long flute of cool champagne.

# THE GENERAL RESTORES ORDER

# 9

THE end of the May 'revolution', its official finish so to speak, might be said to have coincided with (*a*) the massive vote in favour of General de Gaulle's highly personal régime, (*b*) the holding of the *baccalauréat*, confined to a *viva voce*, and the breaking up of the school term, if one can dignify by *term* the occupation by students of classrooms and faculty buildings, and (*c*) a concerted rush by car for the seaside and two months holiday.

The General's dismissal of M. Pompidou, faintly reminiscent of Emperor William II's dismissal of Bismarck, the promise of new taxation, to put France in line with less gold-happy nations, and a good deal of searching self-analysis, lay heavily in the air. Nobody quite understood how it had come to pass that whereas at the beginning 80 per cent of Parisians were apparently in favour of the student riots, the Red Flag waving and anarchy, exactly the same percentage showed itself just as violently in favour of law and order two months later. Half a million people were said to have taken part in the early manifestation organized by the revolutionaries at Denfert-Rochereau; half a million others (or perhaps the same half-million) suddenly decided to march on the Place de la Concorde and up the Champs Elysées, hoist the Tricolour and electrify themselves and their friends with the rousing strains of the 'Marseillaise'. It was all most confusing.

While our village was filling up with holiday makers I was so busy trying to turn a record crop of black and white-hart cherries and redcurrants into jam and ruby-coloured jelly that I found myself neglecting the sands. Could it be that I loved the house and garden more tenderly than ever now that they might at any moment be taken away from me?

One morning, towards the middle of July, Georgette arrived with her tragic air. The hay in our hayfield between the Cour du Cerf and the Picane was cut and rotting on the ground. At the

Burgundy it was trussed, but there was not enough prolonged sunshine to dry it. If things went on like this they would have to buy hay this winter.

With the exception of three days (during two of which I was in Paris) when the temperature was in the eighties, the weather had never been warm enough to tempt one on the sands. We had only bathed once. The result, as far as I was concerned, was merely to make a different sort of summer. Not only did fruit-picking and jam-making take up more of my time, but both the flower garden and the kitchen garden required so much attention that I became happily absorbed in them. By bed time I was exhausted. Digging, planting, weeding, mowing, prevented me from thinking about other things. I persuaded myself that I had achieved something useful.

The country had been so torn by political and social turmoil that the summer, quite apart from the weather, could not help being different. Friends whose husbands were in business had a worried look. They had been told by the new prime minister that it would take eighteen months to make good the damage. New legislation was pending. In addition there was that leap in the dark—workers' participation in management! In the scholastic world, that annual summer headache the *baccalauréat* had assumed political undertones. The fact that it had been based solely on the *viva voce* was in itself an admission on the part of the government that it was anxious to smooth things over by making this impor-tant examination, just for this once, less difficult than usual. The extremists at the Sorbonne and at Nanterre had cried: 'No more examinations!' The government was meeting them half way. So many weeks of the term had been spent at the barricades that book work had obviously suffered. The government would tighten things up later. For the moment peace was what mattered. Thus quite a lot more students than usual received their coveted *baccalauréat*, in fact so many that the authorities began to wonder seriously how they were going to deal with the added influx into the universities. Meanwhile parents whose sons and daughters had been at private religious schools persuaded themselves that more than the usual number of their children had been failed. It was whispered that examiners of pronounced left wing ten-dencies were perhaps getting their own back against the bour-geoisie. For these of course were fee-paying schools. This question mark hung uncomfortably in the damp air of a wet July.

Georgette's passing worries sat lightly on her youthful shoulders. Besides, she was cool and looking quite her best in a new sleeveless dress. To comfort her I exclaimed: 'Oh, Georgette, what a pretty dress!'

Preening herself, she cooed: 'You would never guess. There's a story to it.'

'To the dress?'

'Aunt Marie,' she began, 'Madeleine Déliquaire's sister, who does a bit of charring during the season for the summer residents, looks after a very modern villa in the rue Pasteur.'

'The one that looks like a Swiss chalet owned by some Parisians in the fashion business?'

'She asked her very elegant employer for some bits of old rag to dust with. With all these plastic inventions, and the fact that so many young women have ceased even to sew a button on, odd pieces of material are difficult to come by.

' "No," said her employer, "I don't think I have any rags."

'But Aunt Marie was not going to be put off as easily as that. When she is making things tidy, she likes to have a duster or a soft rag in her hand. So she went on:

' "The best, madame, would be if you had a worn linen sheet, or a cotton sheet with a hole in it that I could turn into dusters?"

' "But my poor Marie," said her employer. "All our sheets are new and of gaily coloured nylon. Far too pretty and expensive to turn into dusters!"

'Cousin Marie went on with her work for a few moments, and then, returning to the attack: "I could probably manage, madame, with one of monsieur's old shirts."

' "Hush, Marie!" her employer cried. "Suppose he were to hear you! No, Marie, his shirts are far too beautiful, but wait, I have an idea."

'A few moments later Aunt Marie's employer came back with this dress. "There," she said, "you can have this to make dusters out of." '

Georgette paused for breath. Her smile was slightly triumphant. She went on:

'Aunt Marie hurried to her sister, Madeleine, who in exchange for the dress gave her a bundle of old rags. My mother-in-law gave the dress to me. I put it in the washing-machine, then on a hanger to dry, and now here it is on my back.'

'How wonderful!' I exclaimed.

But Georgette's expression had suddenly changed to one of indignation.

'How dare these rich people be so wasteful! They are downright wicked, don't you think?'

'If they were mean', I objected, 'you would not have had your pretty dress, and what is more you would have hated them for being mean.'

Georgette's anger turned to laughter and I said to her:

'You are looking unusually pretty this summer. Your arms are dimpled and honey-coloured. Have you never wondered about producing a son for Jacques, and a brother for Brigitte?'

'Oh, Madame Henrey!' she cried. 'Don't even suggest such a thing! I'll soon be forty and they say that when one has a boy at my age he's not likely to do anything very worth while in life! I fancy they get spoilt. It's because at my age there's a bit more money in the bank. The hard years are behind us. Or at least we hope so. A boy at my age! Just think of the fuss we would make of him!'

My friend Yolande paid me one of her lightning visits. She was wearing a very pretty blouse in Tricel, a gay, colourful design on an olive green background. Tall and slim with a tiny blonde head on an elegant long neck, she never seems to grow any older. She was, as usual, bubbling over with news. This time it was of course about her 'revolution'.

Her husband who is an expert in machinery for oil exploration is always travelling to strange countries. So is Yolande, who simply can't stay still. She is like a beautiful, inquisitive bird whose mind is alternately occupied with a new hair-do and how to buy or sell an apartment or a country cottage. She amuses, shocks and bewilders me.

This time she had just come back from Iran where her son had found himself a job with Air France. Back in Paris the 'revolution' had complicated the already involved pattern of her life.

'But', she exclaimed, filling my kitchen (where I was ironing) with the gaiety of her voice and presence, 'for my husband, the revolution was something extraordinary! He suddenly redis-covered the heady joys and recklessness of his youth. In spirit he was back in his early twenties. Take it from me, Madeleine, men are never so happy as during wars, strikes and revolutions. They revel in change. The May 'revolution' and the mini-skirt positively gave them new life!'

'What a wildly exciting juxtaposition!' I said, banging the hot iron on the frilly edges of a nylon pillow case.

'You know that!' she said. 'They are all alike. As for us women, change invariably spells trouble. Don't revolutions and strikes just make you frightened? We women hate upsets. We fear for our homes, our lovely clothes, our possessions and our children. We are always the ones who pay. Whereas my husband last May and June didn't have a worry in the world.

'He is a business executive. Every morning he went to his office and every morning they said to him: "Good morning, sir. We are all on strike."

'So do you know what he did? Leaving the less important members of staff to occupy the office premises, he stepped gaily into the streets of Paris, filled his lungs with the sweet air of chestnut trees in bloom and swung along the boulevards and the avenues doubtless casting appreciative glances at the girls. Tired of walking he would jump into his car. No policemen! No traffic lights! No taxis to get in your way! Cars parked anywhere without their owners running the risk of a fine! What a lovely experience for an executive on a nice May morning!

'One day he was driving along in his 404, drinking in the delights of Paris, when he caught up with a stream of crawling cars. There was a station wagon and several private cars, all creeping along as if their drivers didn't know that there was practically no speed limit any longer in the heart of Paris. My husband hooted (which of course is quite forbidden in normal times) and then, feeling youthful and aggressive, started to put his head out of the window and to abuse the people in front. "Go to school! Learn to drive!"

'After a while a gentleman approached and, putting an index finger to his lips, whispered: "Do please be more respectful, my dear sir. You are in a funeral procession. The undertakers and the gravediggers are all on strike, so we are taking the coffin to the cemetery in the station wagon, and hoping for the best." '

Yolande's finances are of a kind entirely her own. For instance, she wanted to know if I could put her up for a few days in mid August when even the caravan sites are full.

'Of course,' I answered. 'You are always welcome, but what has happened to your own cottage on the estuary of the Seine near Pont Audemer? I thought you always went there in August?'

'That's the point!' she exclaimed. 'This year I have been obliged to let it in order to pay the gardener!'

'Couldn't you have done without a gardener? If you had, you would have had the house!'

'Alas!' she moaned. 'The lawns! One simply has to have well-tended lawns, and they cost a fortune!'

Yolande's incursions into real estate had once before resulted in my having the pleasure of her visit on the farm. On that occasion the transaction called for the sale of the apartment she and her family then occupied in Paris and the purchase of another, presumably larger, more expensive and commodious. At that time it sufficed to buy an apartment at the beginning of the year to sell it at a large profit at the end of the same year. In Yolande's case the new owners arrived punctually on the stipulated day, but, when she and her family sought to take possession of the new apartment, they discovered that the contractors needed another six months to finish the building. There had been strikes, and that was not all. The building had been sold before it was fully erected to a different set of speculators. Yolande found herself temporarily homeless and so to my great joy I had them grouped around me.

Since then I had become the person to whom she flew in similar trouble. She repaid me by an extraordinary affection, an occasional visit and from time to time a letter in which she poured out her adventures, her accidents, her disappointments, her aspirations and her madcap enthusiasms.

Some days after this particular visit, while I was weeding the nasturtiums that every year overrun the rosebeds, two elegant persons got out of their car at the top of the orchard and looked over my fence. I had worked rather well that afternoon, and though I was in no state to receive visitors, especially strangers, I was in excellent humour.

'We are friends of Yolande!' explained the elder of the two women as she handed me something done up in tissue paper.

Inviting my guests to be seated under the coloured umbrellas in the garden, I went to wash the mud off my hands and then opened the package. Inside was the very pretty blouse in Tricel (the one with the gay spots) which she had worn on her recent visit to me and which I had madly admired! With the blouse was a piece of paper on which she had written: 'You admired my blouse. Please accept it with my love!'

That was the sort of person Yolande was! She had greatness in her! She bowled me over by her Spanish courtesy.

She was, I gathered, just then interested in the arts. She was helping to arrange an exhibition of sculpture and painting at Monte Carlo. The elder of the two women, who spoke with a delightful Russian accent, apparently lived in New York, but occasionally spent a season in Paris or Venice. It sounded like Henry James and quite astoundingly remote from my nasturtiums. The Grand Life surprises and enchants me, but I find it hard to believe in. The younger of my two guests was scarcely more than a girl. She wore her hair short like a boy's, but how pretty and feminine were her appealing blue eyes!

I told them how glad I was at the thought that Yolande would be coming to see me in mid August. They told me that she was off to Aix-en-Provence to attend somebody's wedding, then afterwards she would rush off somewhere else to meet her son who was flying home from Teheran. I surmised that before bringing me her family she would doubtless have managed to go half round the world.

As the weather became belatedly warmer, and the summer residents met to gossip and sunbathe at their usual place on the sands, the May 'revolution' began to take on the unreality of a curious, picturesque dream. At Nanterre, shortly after my visit, students of unknown political colour, some said of the extreme Right, some of the extreme Left, broke up the cafeteria, smashed doors, windows, offices, stole books, documents and typewriters, and ransacked the departments of history, geography and psychology!

These 'little darlings', as somebody called the country's university students as a whole, who during the long disturbed months had demonstrated so violently against our modern society of artificially created needs (American style advertising), had run up quite a bill for the replacements they themselves had made necessary. Government experts said that the damage by students in university buildings exceeded £1,000,000, and that this did not take into consideration damage to the Odéon Theatre, looted shops, broken shop windows, sawn-down trees, torn-up paving-stones, cars and lorries set on fire, police vans destroyed! The 'little darlings', whatever they had not learnt at the university, had at least mastered the exhilarating art of making the state disgorge its hard-earned savings!

The state, incidentally, sounded a little sick of them. We were told that all the university buildings would be repainted and whitewashed so that the offending posters and writings on the walls would disappear for ever. Street rioting would not be tolerated! There was not even to be any dancing in the streets of the Left Bank on the 14th July holiday. The Bank of France, like a miser forced to disgorge, had lost a small part of its hard-won gold, and the franc, fighting bravely for its life, was in the humiliating position of often being exchanged abroad at a slight discount. In all this, however, General de Gaulle, his voice clear and vibrant, had lost none of his prestige. He was still the giant in a dazed but confident land. The state television from which, for the moment at any rate, so many of the familiar announcers had disappeared, was falling over its new self in an effort to be polite and factual. One had the curious impression that quite a lot of people would have liked to wipe the whole 'revolution' off the blackboard with one big swish of a damp sponge so that no future historian would be tactless enough to mention it.

The garden beds, insufficiently tended, were suddenly full of weeds, under the rose trees, between the hydrangeas, at the foot of the sweet peas; and in the kitchen garden, where I struggled practically alone against every form of adversity, the early potatoes needed digging up, the final rows of leeks and beetroots planted. I felt like Eve alone in the garden of Eden.

To the right of my white entrance gate, at the top of M. Levannier's orchard, tents and caravans had once more appeared. Georgette informed me that they were the same people who had planted their tents there the previous summer, and that they were from M. Levannier's native part of France. Though their colourful encampment would remain all summer, they might only come for week-ends. The sands over Saturday and Sunday were the attraction. In short, they would enjoy the advantages of a villa by the sea without having to buy or rent one. The prohibitive cost of life beside the seaside was no myth. Every time they came they would bring with them in the car (or cars) all their food and everything they would need. Everything except milk, which they would collect at milking time from M. Levannier, and bread which they would buy in the village when they went down to bathe. The previous summer I had rather resented this vulgarization of our peaceful countryside. Since the menace of the road I no longer cared. What was the noise of a few campers to the uprooting of an entire way of life? Besides, the 'revolution' of May had intellectually made me quite another woman. I felt less of a participator, more of a spectator. Most of my women friends felt the same. Events had gone beyond us. There was nothing we could do about changes of such magnitude. I felt like Andrée when her boys disobeyed her. They were physically and aggressively the stronger. Not only to our orchards and leafy lanes did strangers come with their packaged food. To Paris, deserted by warm-hearted, generous spending American and British tourists, were now coming hordes of visitors from behind the Iron Curtain whose expenses had all been met in their own currency before leaving Moscow, Leningrad, Bucharest or Prague. No shopkeeper, no taxi-driver would benefit from their closely supervised Intourist visit. They could gape but not spend.

Our village had of course been hitherto hopelessly old-fashioned. We had not even discovered the joys of traffic lights, but now that traffic tended to speed through us rather than to us, these had become, at least to our local police force, a delightful necessity. Our meandering village streets became one-way streets with traffic plunging down one hill, roaring up the other, while we scarcely dared to cross a road to buy a reel of cotton or an ounce of knitting wool. When I was a young married woman we had a flat in London, near Harrods, at the corner of Beauchamp Place and Brompton Road. How old-fashioned it all seemed until the grind of brakes, the changing of gears and the escape of exhaust followed the advent of the traffic lights!

As July gave way to August market days brought us something of the bustle and colour of what one still loved best in France. The peaches, the melons, the first sweet grapes from the vineyards, the tomatoes, the late cherries and early pears covered the stalls in turbulent array. There was too much of everything.

One of the effects of the Common Market was to oblige fruit farmers in the Midi to destroy the surplus of their crops so that prices could be maintained. Tons of peaches, tomatoes and melons were thrown on the main motor roads by growers protesting at this example of man's folly. Lorry drivers and passing motorists were given as much fruit as they could eat and then told to drive their vehicles over torrents of luscious fruit that crazy politicians had committed to destruction.

To Georgette's delight and mine, however, our market was also full of bright jersey dresses from Italy at ten francs each. A pretty salesgirl wore one of them herself, and I was tempted to buy one of the same kind that she displayed so seductively herself. Nothing is more conducive to optimism than the sudden, on the spur of the moment purchase of an uproariously gay summer dress at a bargain price. All my day was to be filled with sunshine.

The cowbell on my garden gate tinkled. I ran out and discovered Jacqueline, a young professor of English in a big girls' school who was on her way to catch the night boat at Le Havre. She had had the excellent idea of looking in on me and, as I knew she had been in the centre of student trouble ever since May, I was doubly glad to see her. 'All those girls', I said to her 'between the ages of twelve and sixteen! What did they do? Were you also on strike?'

'But I never went on strike,' she exclaimed over strawberry jam and China tea, 'or at least not voluntarily! If it had been a question of solidarity over wages, supposing we had been inadequately paid, I would have been whole-heartedly with my colleagues, but it was never a question of money. The whole thing, as far as our school was concerned, was political. The trouble was that I felt pretty satisfied with my lot, could not think of any claims I wanted to advance, and had no political views whatsoever. In the end, of course, I became of necessity involved, but I lost face with my colleagues who for a time were scarcely polite to me. There was a day when one suffered for one's religious beliefs. Now it is for one's lack of conformity.

'Our girls were a little young to become embroiled in ideology. The mistresses doubtless received their instructions from university cells. Those who wavered were gradually won over. They had no reason to make themselves martyrs. What would you have done in their place if you had been a young woman in the teaching profession? I am really not sure what came over me. My husband, who is honesty in person, exclaimed: "Why on earth make yourself ill? Do like everybody else."

'We knew all about the events at Nanterre, how on 8th January the Minister in charge of Youth, M. François Missoffe, declaring open the big swimming-pool bordering the campus, had that now famous altercation with a then utterly unknown student.

' "I have read your white paper on youth!" the student, according to newspaper reports, cried out. "You don't even mention the sex problems of youth in it!"

' "At your age," the Minister is said to have answered, "I didn't need to study a white paper to know about that!"

'There was another aspect of the Nanterre unrest which reached our ears, the fact that in the early part of the Easter term one hundred Chinese students, under the government's cultural agreement, spent a month at Nanterre University. This and certain films shown in Paris charged the air with political pollen.

'How did all this affect us women teachers?

'I can only tell you how it came down to me personally.

'I was starting an English literature class one morning when a girl of fourteen put up her arm and interrupted me:

' "What is it?" I asked, vexed to be put off my subject.

' "We would like to talk to you, miss!"

' "Couldn't it wait till after the class?" I asked. "Today's lesson is rather important."

' "No," said the little girl. "It's urgent."

' "Very well," I said reluctantly. "Stand up in front of your desk and tell me what it is."

'The little girl looked at me with candid blue eyes and said:

' "We want you to give us a course in sexual education."

' "That's not my department," I said. "I'm an English literature mistress. You will have to see the headmistress. What do you want to know about sex?"

' "Could you tell us about the Pill?"

' "You know as well as I do that the law requires your father's permission, and as none of you in this class is yet eighteen years of age I can't see what is so urgent about your question. Couldn't it have waited till the end of the lesson? You were not planning to take the Pill tonight, I suppose?"

'A titter of laughter saved me from this awkward situation, but from that day onwards my girls had an air of buzzing round me like a swarm of bees round a honey jar. I could sense trouble on the way. They were proud to have obliged me to "dialogue" about sex. As they were all so young and I not so very much older, I sympathized with them. Nevertheless I was an English literature mistress and my job was to see that they passed their exams.

'Unrest was spreading amongst the mistresses themselves, and, because my neutral attitude annoyed them, I was made to feel cold-shouldered. Many of them, for instance, pretended to look the other way when I bade them good morning. I needed the morning off to attend a funeral. The headmistress was in conference with some of my colleagues, but, interrupting them, I asked very politely for the usual permission. She looked annoyed.

' "There are no funerals because of the strike," she said.

'I answered with equal conviction: "This one is certainly taking place. The procession is already forming, and what is more they are carrying the Tricolour flag, as they always do for an ex-soldier of the 1914–18 war."

' "Very well," said the headmistress. "If that is the case."

'My next class was to be the last before the school became idle. I was due to take some of the older girls whose normal professor I knew to be extremely left wing. There was a good deal of laughter as I opened the door, but it ceased as I approached the rostrum. I stood in front of the class for a few moments looking searchingly at the girls who appeared polite but agitated.

'At last they all began whispering at once: "Look at the blackboard, miss, look at the blackboard!"

'I hesitated before turning round. I really had not looked at the blackboard or perhaps, more accurately, I had probably looked at it without seeing it, as so often happens.

'So I turned slowly and nervously round. What terrible thing would I see? Well, believe it or not, the entire blackboard which took up most of the wall behind my rostrum, was covered with these words written over and over again at every imaginable angle so that the wall looked like an immense tapestry. This is what it said at least one thousand times: "We want to talk to you, miss!" "We want to talk to you, miss!" "We want to talk to you, miss!"

' "Oh!" I exclaimed involuntarily. "The idea is Chinese!"

' "Oh yes," they cried. "It's Mao."

' "I think you should all begin by cleaning the blackboard," I said. "Afterwards, we will talk."

' "Very well, miss."

'So very good-humouredly, they cleaned the blackboard.

' "And now," I asked, "what are we going to talk about?"

' "We want a cafeteria," they said.

' "That sounds reasonable, but why ask me. You must apply to the finance committee."

' "We would like a senior girls' room where we can be together during recreation time."

' "What else do you want?"

' "We want our own girls' club."

' "How strange," I said. "Only a short time ago when your classes were over you ran off to amuse yourselves in the big world. Now, even in your recreation time, you want to stay among girls in your study room or your club. But, alas, all this is no business of mine. Are we to work today or are you girls already taking over?"

'In fact they had taken over.'

Now here we were once again at the height of the short Deauville season, a toned-down, democratic echo of the once fashionable Grande Semaine when authors, film stars, actresses, painters and millionaire racehorse owners displayed themselves at the Bar du Soleil or in the marble hall of the Normandy Hotel. Anticipating September and the opening of the shooting season, French sportsmen were being invited in catalogues and shop windows to admire forthcoming styles for *la chasse*. Newspapers depicted men with strong jaws and virile features wearing Sherlock Holmes caps, tweedy clothes and stout boots all equipped with shotguns, bandoleers and briar pipes to shoot whatever still moved between non-existent hedges or over chemically manured fields. The robins that forsook me in summer, sensing the smell of gunpowder in the woods, timidly arrived in my garden to feed with the tits, the sparrows and the jays. Georgette arrived bearing me a gift of a hen with four baby

powder-puff chicks that immediately hid themselves under their
mother's wings. No two powder puffs looked alike, one being
white, the second black, the third bronze and the fourth grey. I
had almost forgotten what lessons a mother hen was capable of
giving the human race. Her devotion and watchfulness were
touching, but so also was the instinctive obedience of her young.
The stately walnut trees I planted over ten years ago on either
side of the lane, whose hedges had been too severely cut down,
were already forming a leafy arch to produce shade, and the
boughs were full of walnuts. I had been so sure that somebody
half a century hence would enjoy their majestic splendour. Alas,
they were in the way of the projected motor road and would
doubtless be ground down by the bulldozer.

M. Salesse, the schoolmaster, had called on me the other day.
'I know it's going to happen,' he said, 'but out of bravado I have
just bought one of the most menaced orchards at the back of my
house, and not cheaply either. I intend to hold my head high
till the last moment and maybe, who can tell, I shall never see it!'

The plum trees were full of the sort of plums that farmers
farther south were throwing on the high roads for lorries and
cars to run over because of Common Market folly, but which
sold in the shops for the equivalent of 2s. a pound. Having made
jam of some and stewed others, I filled a great basket to take as a
gift to my friend Mme Durville at her villa in the heart of the
village.

The news of Russian tanks thundering across Czechoslovakia,
entering the proud city of Prague, had sent unpleasant tremors
down the spines of television viewers taught to believe that the
Russians were easier for France to do business with than the
warmongering Americans. Now where did everybody stand?
Thank goodness, the weather had suddenly turned warm and it
was hot enough to lie on the sands or even to bathe.

Mme Durville was out. She and her husband, the doctor, were
exercising their pekinese who, with his poor flat nose so near the
ground, found our seaside village much better for his canine
lungs than the streets of Paris, even in the smartest district of the
capital.

'Ah, madame!' exclaimed Sophia, Mme Durville's Polish
maid. 'Madame will be delighted with the plums. The dear
doctor is very fond of fruit.'

The morning paper lay on the kitchen table among the carrots and the apples she was preparing for lunch. The headlines screamed the terror of the people in Prague seeing the first Russian tanks.

'What times we are once again living through,' said Sophia, making a helpless gesture in the direction of the paper. 'For me, a Pole, they are tragically poignant, for has not my unfortunate country, that never harmed any other nation, bled more than most from the brutalities of the invader?

'I have been in France since before the last war. In the summer of 1939 my eldest daughter who had gone to Poland for a holiday with my parents was caught when Hitler sent those fifty-four first line divisions into Poland. Then the Russians, violating their non-aggression pact, poured in through our eastern frontier. The Nazi bombers started their systematic obliteration of Warsaw. Imagine, madame, how I felt!

'My daughter came back to me after the liberation, a young girl who no longer knew what it was to laugh or even to smile.

' "Do you know, Mother," she said, "that a poor little Jewish boy once came to Granny's house, throwing himself at her feet and sobbing:

' " 'Dear lady, for the love of God, take me in. Put me with your pigs in the pigsty. I'll feed on what they leave and I'll sleep with them. But I shall be in somebody's home, even though I'm with your animals. I'll not be alone any longer, for I have no home and not a relative left in the world.' "

' "Granny said: 'Alas, everybody in the village knows that I'm so poor I couldn't afford to pay a child to look after my pigs. And soon they are coming to take my pigs away from me and then what would happen to you?' "

' "As she spoke we heard the sound of tramping feet. A Nazi soldier hit the boy on the head with the butt of his rifle, cracking his poor little skull right open, and we were left to bury him. Shall I tell you what the Germans were like in Poland, Mother? A woman who lived in our street was wheeling her pram with her baby daughter in it when some German soldiers came along. They swore at her because she didn't get out of their way quickly enough. One of them took the baby girl out of the pram and throwing her on the pavement stamped on her with his jack-boots."

'This is what my daughter had to tell me when she came back from Poland.

'My poor little mother, also, who was picking up beetroot in a field was hit by a Russian bullet. She had time to look up and see the postman coming along the lane.

' "Oh, postman!" she cried. "Are you bringing me a letter from my daughter in France?"

'He shook his head negatively, and she collapsed and died.'

On the sands, because the weather was suddenly so beautifully warm, almost for the first time that summer all the regular summer residents were sunbathing and exchanging gossip.

'I have been so terribly busy,' said the elegant mother of a teenage daughter. 'Our new apartment in the XVIth *arrondissement* in Paris is nearly finished. The fitted carpets are all in place and the building is so modern that when we drive into the private garage, a special lift takes us straight up to the apartment. Undoubtedly there is a great satisfaction in having a place of our own in a district of Paris as fashionable as Passy. And what a splendid investment! I'm sure it will be twice as valuable in a few years time. I'm madly happy!'

I plunged into the sea, so cold, calm and clear, to soothe my vaguely troubled thoughts. This evening I would drive into Deauville to mix with the crowd. Or perhaps stay at home and watch television which was to have a long feature on autumn fashions with interviews with the leading Paris dress designers. I chose television. These serious frivolities were to be followed by a play by Calderón de la Barca which would be exquisitely acted.

Top Paris models, wearing dresses of geometrical design, were photographed upside-down, sideways, their heads cut off from their shoulders, their legs without the rest of their bodies. Television and fashion photographers were so anxious to display their artistic nonconformity and genius that one had the impression that both the models and the dresses had ceased to matter. I turned with relief to the love intrigues and delightful dialogue of the play by Calderón, the future canon of Toledo, and marvelled at the importance in those days that men attached to women. After midnight, however, owing to the heat, I was on edge, nerves taut, perhaps because I kept remembering what Sophia had said.

At last I fell asleep, but shortly after six I heard through my sleep a voice calling me. Sensing some tragedy I ran to the open window, leaned out of it and saw Georgette standing in the middle of the garden path looking up expectantly. The morning was cool and a mist was coming up from the sea.

'Madame Henrey!' cried Georgette in her small voice. 'Monsieur Paul has hanged himself from a beam in the attic of mother's place!'

'Oh, the poor man! The poor man!' I found myself repeating.

Monsieur Paul, a sort of uncle by adoption, had been staying with Rosalie, Georgette's Ukrainian-born mother, in her cottage on the other side of the railway line. During the 'revolution' of May he had been taken in an ambulance to hospital at Caen, and later, after the usual operation, allowed to return home.

Still leaning out of the window, too shaken to think of running down to Georgette in my nightdress, I waited. She said:

'He had an argument with the doctor who told him that he must try to bear the pain, great as it was, a few days longer because, alas, it was bound to get worse, and then he would have to be given massive injections. There was not only the pain, there was the humiliation. A man who had been so proud of his neat appearance, so anxious never to give the slightest trouble to others! He became so ashamed. He insisted on the doctor telling him the truth. "It's cancer, isn't it, doctor? How much longer have I to live?" All yesterday morning he had asked mother what she was doing at home. Why did she not go to work? What prevented her from going down to the village to do the shopping. He wanted to get her out of the way. At last, reluctantly, she left. First he tried to asphyxiate himself. Then he changed his mind and, though he could hardly drag himself about, climbed to the attic where he tied a rope to a beam, making a loop for his neck. The roof was so low what when Rosalie found him hanging there was scarcely any space between his feet and the floor.'

'The poor, poor man!' I repeated.

'The humiliation and the pain were too much,' said Georgette. 'I used to find him in tears. It's terrible to see a man in tears.'

'I think he was rather brave,' I said.

She left and the news from Prague filled the air, filled the quiet

garden where the robin was waiting for his plate of bread and
milk. The French Government was cleaning the slogans off the
walls of the new university at Nanterre and at the Sorbonne;
children were drawing water from the pump at the shanty town
not half a mile from Nanterre University's magnificent new
swimming-pool, Deauville was getting ready for the Grand
Prix, and down in the village the church bell was tolling for
Monsieur Paul's release from earthly pain.

What business had I to worry about the threat of a motorway
to my house and garden? If only the sun would break through
the morning mist I would run down to the sands and bathe.

Soon autumn would be with us.

As September came upon us, with its hedges bearing autumnal
gifts of hazel nuts and blackberries, mothers in our village turned
their minds anxiously to the reopening of schools and universities. Though her school, in common with others, opened late,
Brigitte was soon happily back with her classmates. Universities
presented a more hazardous problem. The government hesitated.
Would there be trouble? Was it ready to meet it? Most people
expected a winter of discontent. They were resigned to the thought
that there must be some violent echo of the 'revolution' of May,
but as man's imagination is limited, the most generally held view
was that any trouble that happened was bound to break out as
before in the academic world. In November a new and intense
crisis came. The General claimed it may have had its origins in
the events of May, but it took place in a sphere so different from
that of schools and universities that once again the whole nation
was taken by surprise. It happened in a sphere in which up to
now there had been such confidence, such pride, such almost
unique freedom.

Some weeks earlier I had been made miserable by a chill
caught on the beach during one of those sudden squalls that
obliterate the sun in a matter of seconds during the lovely but
misleading weather of an Indian summer. The bathing tents had
been removed, nearly all the summer residents had gone, first
the husbands then the wives with children preparing for the new
school term. Many of the shops were closed, shopkeepers choosing
this moment to go off for their own holidays, to Italy, to Spain,
even to England, foreign holidays being very much in the air,
almost a necessity to keep up one's social standing. My husband

had dropped me at the sands where it was my intention to bathe under a pleasantly hot sun. In fact the sea proved rougher than I expected, the sky suddenly became black, and while wearing only a swimsuit and a bathrobe I was caught in a downpour while waiting for the car to return. When it finally came I was shivering, coughing and furious.

A day or two later, while I was preparing breakfast, a young man appeared at the kitchen door, holding a tall rolled-up parchment tied at the centre with a red tape. Sniffing my coffee, he said amiably: 'Madam, I am a geologist from the Ministry of Bridges and Highways and I head a team of experts surveying the sub-structure of the soil over which the new road is planned to run.'

With the kettle still poised over the percolator I said thoughtfully: 'So there is going to be a road. I was not quite sure.'

'Yes,' answered the young man, 'depending, of course, on what we find. We have a machine with us that sends a shaft down to a depth of some eighty feet. It brings up samples from each layer. Have you any idea what your sub-soil is like?'

'Vaguely. I remember, for instance, that when our well was being sunk before the war, the men found a treacherous layer of black sand some forty feet down. One of them working at the bottom was nearly asphyxiated. He was unconscious when we hauled him up.'

'Have you any objection, madam, if we run a shaft down?' He smiled. 'It will scarcely leave a trace. Just like a needle piercing your flesh.'

'The simile is apt,' I said. 'As for my permission I doubt if I have any choice. Where do you propose to do it?'

'Between the white gates of your orchard and your tenants' farmhouse.'

'So much to the west?' I queried. 'I thought——'

'That was the original idea. The new plan is to be on a much grander scale. Instead of being on a glorified by-pass you are now to be part of the great Paris–Normandy autoroute, of its western arm, one of the largest and most modern autoroutes in all Europe!'

There was pride in his youthful voice. He went on enthused: 'The arm to Rouen is nearly completed. Work on this one, the arm to Caen, will doubtless begin in the early seventies. It will cost a fabulous sum.'

'Will it still run through the centre of my house?'

'No, madam. There is a deviation. Oh, not a very big one, but of extreme importance. It will virtually cut off a corner of your living-room and then run like an arrow over those two orchards to within an inch or two of your tenant farmer's farmhouse. Right through his cider press, I would think.'

'How charming. So I will not only lose my own house but also the farm and all its buildings?'

'Yes,' agreed the young man. 'Would you like to see the map?'

'That thing you are holding like a marshal's baton?'

'I could unroll for you the part that crosses your estate?'

'You could perhaps lay it out on the table in the big room,' I said, 'the table in front of the stone pillars of the sixteenth-century fireplace. You could even leave it there while you go about your business. I will ask my husband to telephone to our neighbour, M. Phillip Pradeau, who will be interested, and also to our local schoolmaster, M. Salesse, a town councillor, who is very worried about his own house and the house he is building for his daughter. It will not make them any happier, but it will be a courtesy all the same. You have no objection, I take it?'

'None,' said the young man.

Later, while a lorry carrying the machinery, followed by a fleet of cars, passed along the lane on the way to Georgette's farm, we stood in the garden computing the exact path of the proposed autoroute. Yes, if this plan did come into being, not only would our house and garden be engulfed but also the orchard belonging to Mme Bompain, the farmhouse in which Georgette, Jacques and Brigitte lived, all the farm buildings and two more orchards beyond. The immense autoroute, according to this new detailed plan, would run westward to Caen, three to four miles inland, through woods, meadows and hills. There would be cuttings and an occasional tunnel. The present modern road from Deauville to Caen would become superfluous. What millions of francs the country must possess to indulge in such apparent luxuries! There seemed altogether too much money about!

I accompanied the men as far as Georgette's place and then left them to their men's talk. I borrowed a plastic pail from Georgette and started picking blackberries. More than ever I felt an urge to take what I could from the land before the great massacre. There was a warm sun, and a dozen cows in M. Levannier's orchard ambled towards me, delightfully unconscious of all these busy human plans for destruction. This was a man's world and there was nothing that Georgette or I could do about it. 'Well, at least,' said Georgette, 'we must hope the winter school term doesn't bring us another revolution. Everybody is so afraid, so much on edge this autumn.'

'There was a time', I said (mostly to myself) 'when the beginning of autumn promised new plays, new books, the autumn collections of the big Paris dressmakers. Well, obviously things must change.'

My cold got no better during the next few days and a tooth that should have been attended to earlier was now painful. I was curiously mistrustful of new dentists, but it seemed absurd to go to London merely to keep a dentist's appointment when Caen with its teaching hospitals had men of great repute.

Caen is a city that has risen brashly from the ruins of tank battles and aerial bombardments. The speed of the rebuilding gives it a shoddy air, and its inhabitants complain that like so many other modern cities it is without character or life at night. As soon as the shops and supermarkets close, people retire indoors to watch television. My dentist was on the first floor of a large new building in one of the busiest streets where the noise of traffic, the smell of roasting coffee beans and the throng of shoppers gave it a certain gaiety. On the other side of the street was a huge supermarket. The dentist's waiting-room had thin walls and a tall french window that overlooked the courtyard in which a few cars were parked. One had glimpses of slippered women in upper apartments watering tubs of wilted plants, hanging out washing, feeding canaries in cages. Nothing looked very romantic or conversely solid. The picturesque character of the medieval, destroyed city was missing. Two cheap modern pictures in cream frames hung on the walls, and there were the usual much-thumbed magazines on a narrow table between two rows of chairs against opposing walls. A girl was ushered in and after a while I kept on meeting her eyes that appeared fascinated by the English language newspaper I had taken out of my bag to read. After a while she said:

'Is that an English newspaper?'

'Yes.'

'Can one obtain it here?'

'I think so. Why do you ask?'

'I'm trying so hard to learn the language. So many girls of my age are going to England, even from the village where we live. This freedom to travel is quite wonderful.'

'Where is your village?'

'Some twenty miles from here. I came in by train, but as the next train back is not till past midday I walked straight here in spite of the fact that my appointment is not for an hour. I have brought a book to read.'

The dentist in his white coat was slim and long legged with dark hair just beginning to grey on the temples. The equipment in front of the huge window above the busy street was blindingly white. Some of it was German, some American, everything ultra-modern. This youthful man with his bright, dark, laughing eyes and delicate hands with long, narrow fingers danced over the slippery floor with the fleetness of a Nureyev, and all the while he kept up a sort of low monologue interrupted from time to time with ejaculations that begged encouraging smiles or nodding assent from his patient. One needed a moment to tune in to his wave-length. His diagnosis was so rapid that once having decided what to do he got on with it while at the same time talking delightfully and intimately about himself, about his family, his politics, his personal problems.

He had worked in England during the war, later throwing himself so untiringly into dental research and new methods of dental surgery that he had suffered a heart attack, and for a time had suddenly found himself obliged to live at half speed, no longer allowed to smoke or to do anything in excess. He came of Breton stock and sailing was his relaxation, his joy. The only photograph on the neat metal writing desk was of his sailing boat. He shared it with a friend, and this past summer they had taken it to St Jean de Luz. In mid August, when all France was on holiday and while they were scudding merrily before a favourable wind, his friend's wife was suddenly taken ill. At the very moment when they needed doctors, specialists and swift transport, the paralysing effects of a modern nation on holiday struck panic into them. They felt helpless, not like men who have passed most of their lives in great hospitals, but like anxious, bewildered members of the non-medical public. 'She is very young, very beautiful and so very gay. We got her as quickly as we could to Paris where she was operated on by that great surgeon who is so close to General de Gaulle.'

I came back the following week and this time heard all about his sons, one of whom had been at the university in Paris during the 'revolution' of May and who was now beset by the complications of growing up and presenting great human problems, as sons always do for their parents. He talked about a thousand things while he swivelled gently round on his leather stool, putting on his spectacles, taking them off again, choosing an instrument, waiting for his girl assistant in the white dress to bring him something he needed. He referred, for example, to Jackie Kennedy's engagement to the Greek shipowner Onassis. This made him quite mad. 'We all worshipped her husband,' he exclaimed, 'so that after his assassination, in our imagination we took her lovingly under our strong male protection. Now she is about to be ravished!' From this subject he turned to the changing attitude of doctors in Paris who refused to be disturbed from their sleep at night, to the future of the Common Market into which it was vital to bring Britain, to the General's dream of turning Paris into the financial hub that London had once been, to the hysteria that Frenchmen were showing at the mere thought that death duties, now almost non-existent, might be raised to pay for the trouble in May.

I left him intrigued by all the things he had said, delighted by what he had done for me. I suddenly felt as glamorous as a film star, and though his fee seemed ruinous I supposed it was not much different from what I would have paid in New York. I wondered whether the little girl I had met in the waiting-room had enjoyed reading my English newspaper and if she would manage to visit London as so many young people dreamed of doing just now. I drove through the outskirts of Caen along the banks of the canal, feeling thoroughly relaxed, past the great cement works between fields of beetroot touched by an early November sun, gladdened by what I had read in the paper, that French industry was catching up with so many lost hours occasioned by the strikes, thinking in my feminine naïveté that all must now be well.

The great money crisis puzzled the people in our village, for just as everything was settling down nicely, the events of May conveniently forgotten, here was the French franc, the heavy franc, symbol of the nation's pride, hit by the icy winds of late November. What malevolent enchanter had whistled away all those comforting gold bars from the vaults of the Bank of France?

But once again the giant roared. The franc would not be devalued. When a nation ceased to work for weeks on end, said the familiar voice over the radio, when trains, ships and public transport stopped, when miners ceased to dig coal and there were no postal services, no radio, no petrol, no electricity, when a balanced budget was thrown by wage demands into imbalance—then even if it was rescued, as France had been rescued, on the edge of an abyss, a nation could only recover its equilibrium by degrees.

Even the most humble people in our village held their heads higher after this unexpected decision and once again life returned to normality.

I also began to feel a great deal better about the road. Not that I believed as some people did that because of the great economy wave, the road would not be built, but because now that the initial shock was over I had become more reasonable, more aware of the transiency of everything I owned.

Besides, the authorities kept on changing their minds. The thing had started the previous Easter with the map M. Salesse, the schoolmaster, had shown me at the town hall. The road as it was then envisaged was to be a by-pass merely cutting off the awkward corner of our village. Later there was this much more important national scheme whereby we would have formed part of the great Paris–Normandy autoroute, one of the largest in Europe. That had been the reason for the geologist's visit, all those soundings between my house and my farmers' houses. Since then I had cause to believe that because of the difficulty of the terrain, the autoroute which would undoubtedly be finished, whatever other cuts were made in government expenditure, would be re-routed farther inland, but this welcome news did not, alas, put an end to the whole sorry story. The local authorities came up again with their obstinate clamour for a by-pass. Momentarily it appeared they had no money. As Maître Vincent had originally said with his cunning smile: 'It's not for just yet. Oh no, not for just yet.'

As in the nursery rhyme one could repeat hopefully: 'This year, next year, some time, never.'

I think perhaps, if I was truly honest with myself, I would have to admit that my passing troubles, however large, however small, were all bound up with the extent of my physical energy. When I hated the wintry countrified scene, all the incredible beauty of our naked orchards, when I longed with all my heart for the bustle and the colour of the town, for those streets of London paved with excitement, I could generally be certain of calming down my nerves by digging the garden or starting a bonfire. How furiously on these occasions did I long for greater strength, greater agility, more energy to match my will-power!

Sometimes on these December evenings after I had cut down the boughs of a dead apple tree whose mossy wood sprouted mistletoe I would build up a splendid bonfire whose smoke and flames rose vigorously into the darkening sky. Then as I gazed through this crackling furnace of dried leaves and twigs I would see M. Levannier on the other side of the hedge running lightly, slim as an athlete, a long perch in his hand, rounding up the cows because it was milking time. How I envied him his strength, his youth and the infectious gaiety of his smile! There, hurrying after him, came his pretty young wife and the two pixies in red.

The last days before Christmas brought me sad news from Andrée Pradeau. Her distinguished father, Dr Salmont, the young soldier whose photograph taken during the First World War I had admired in her workroom at 'Bois Lurette', the aged doctor I had gone over to welcome at the Church of St John the Baptist at Neuilly, when he and his American-born wife were standing by the altar rail before Danièle's wedding, was dead. Andrée's grief was immense and I truly wept for her—for Mme Salmont also, who would now mourn a husband as well as an only son.

Andrée told me she had already broken the news to her bailiff farmer, M. Dénos, whose tyre had so absurdly burst outside the church when he and his family had arrived in their Sunday best for Danièle's wedding. There was something charmingly old-fashioned in the deep mutual affection between the Salmonts and the Pradeaus and their farmer, which occasionally reminded me of some pastoral scene in an eighteenth-century English novel. The sheep in their pens, the children on the back of the milking donkey, the potting sheds, the magnificent trees, the hay-cutting and threshing machines in summer—all these pictures of an almost forgotten world.

The farmers would leave for Paris immediately after milking time the next morning, Andrée told me over the telephone.

M. Dénos, a powerfully set man who could cleave a great elm log with one mighty swing of a sledge-hammer but whose smile was as gentle and as winning as a girl's, was all ready to leave with his wife for Paris. The little car stood in the drive outside the open door of the long low farmhouse which with the stables and the hayricks were at the far end of the park. The weather, with Christmas only a few days off, was cold and M. Dénos had gone out to chop some wood for the fire in the house so that when they returned in the evening the living-room and the kitchen would be warm.

The axe came down with a sharp, dry crack on the chopping block, and the wood, caught at an angle, flew apart, sending a minute splinter into the burly farmer's eye, causing him like Cyclops to emit a great roar of pain which brought his wife flying out of the house. His two large, rough hands were held tightly to the injured eye. When momentarily he released them, the damage was such that Mme Dénos, out of her mind, let out a long panic-stricken wail: 'Oh!' she cried, 'you've gouged it out!'

An operation was carried out at the clinic at Deauville, that same clinic to which Georgette was taken before Brigitte's First Communion and where we had all gone to visit her. The surgeon was hopeful that M. Dénos would recover at least 5 per cent of vision in the injured eye.

Meanwhile at the Levannier's place, the so very youthful, good-looking M. Levannier suddenly, and for no reason at all that he could think of, felt extraordinarily tired. Had he been working too hard? But he was so active, so young, so strong. He sat puzzled and a little pathetic in a corner of his gleaming kitchen, newly painted, the kitchen range warm and inviting, his wife and children round him. When at his wife's bidding the doctor came the young farmer was put immediately to bed and told he must remain as motionless as possible, taking the strain away from his heart. Thus he lay there for the next few days while the bustle of the busy farm, looked after by his wife, by Jacques and by Georgette, went on all around him.

I saw him towards the end of January standing in the sunshine outside the tall brick farmhouse, and when I exclaimed at the joy I felt to see him up and about again, he said very softly, as if in utter bewilderment: 'But why did it have to happen to me, to me who am so young? Had I been older it would have been understandable.'

The lawn in front of my own house was already full of snowdrops, and in the hedge between my kitchen garden and M. Levannier's meadow, the meadow he had made by cutting down all those cider apple trees, the first primroses and cowslips were already in flower.

Thus the long winter is nearly over, and soon one entire year will have gone by since I went to buy a newspaper down in the village and first learnt about the projected road.

Easter will see a rebirth of this lovely land, and may our troubles be behind us.

Villers-sur-Mer
1st February 1969

## DATE DUE

GAYLORD                    PRINTED IN U.S.A.